Collins
E A P

Numbers

Data and statistics

for the non-specialist

Louis Rogers and Dawn Willoughby

Academic Skills Series

Collins

HarperCollins Publishers
77-85 Fulham Palace Road
Hammersmith
London W6 8JB

First edition 2013

Reprint 10 9 8 7 6 5 4 3 2 1 0

© HarperCollins Publishers 2013

ISBN 978-0-00-750715-3

Collins® is a registered trademark of HarperCollins
Publishers Limited

www.collinselt.com

A catalogue record for this book is available from the
British Library

Typeset in India by Aptara

Printed in China by South China Printing Co.

⫐ You can trust Collins COBUILD

The 4.5-billion-word Collins Corpus is the world's largest
database of the English language. It is updated every
month and has been at the heart of Collins COBUILD
publishing for over 20 years. All definitions provided in
the glossary boxes in this book have been taken from the
Collins COBUILD Advanced Dictionary.

About the author

Dawn Willoughby is a qualified teacher in Mathematics. She has taught Statistics to international foundation-level students and undergraduates for the past eight years, on a range of programmes in Business, Information Systems and Statistics, Psychology and Mathematics.

Acknowledgements

I would like to thank my co-author Louis Rogers for being very easy to work with, and I am so grateful for the patience and support of my boys, Matt and Alexander – may their numbers always be correct!

About the author

Louis Rogers has taught English for Academic Purposes and study skills courses at the University of Reading, Nottingham Trent and in Germany for some years. He has authored a number of EFL publications, including many titles in EAP.

Acknowledgements

I would like to offer thanks to my co-author Dawn Willoughby for her support and help in writing the course, and for the patience and support of my family: Cathy, Ruby and Lenny.

We are both grateful to the team at HarperCollins, in particular our editor Daniel Rolph.

Contents

POWERED BY COBUILD

Introduction

Collins Academic Skills Series: Numbers will give you the skills you need for doing research, collecting data, presenting it, using numbers and appropriate language to describe it, and working with the collected data.

Designed to be used on a self-study basis to support English for Academic Purposes or study skills courses, it is intended for students on pre-sessional or foundation courses as well as for first-year undergraduate students.

The book has twelve chapters covering the key stages of the research process from start to finish. You will learn how to:

- choose the right research methods
- use basic maths skills
- present your data
- analyse your data

At the back of the book there is:

- a list of useful books in Further reading
- helpful information in The grammar of fractions
- a Glossary of key terms
- a comprehensive Answer key

Chapter structure

Each chapter includes:

- Aims – These set out the skills covered in the chapter.
- A self-evaluation quiz – By doing this you are able identify what you already know on the subject of the chapter and what you need to learn.
- Information on academic guidelines on how to develop academic skills – These sections will help you understand university practices and expectations so you know what is required.
- Practical exercises – These help you to develop the skills to succeed at university. You can check your answers at the back of the book.
- Tips – Key points are highlighted for easy reference and provide useful revision summaries for the busy student.
- Glossary – Difficult words are glossed in boxes next to where the word appears in the chapter. There is also a comprehensive Glossary at the back of the book.
- Remember sections – This is a summary of key points for revision and easy reference.

Glossary boxes ⒸPOWERED BY COBUILD

Where we feel that a word or phrase is difficult to understand, we have glossed this word/ phrase. All definitions provided in the glossary boxes have been taken from the *COBUILD Advanced Dictionary*. At the end of the book there is a full alphabetical list of the most difficult words from the book for your reference.

Using Numbers

You can either work through the chapters from Chapter 1 to Chapter 12 or you can choose the chapters and topics that are most useful to you. The Contents page will help in your selection.

Study tips

- Each chapter will take between one and three hours. Take regular breaks and do not try to study for too long. Thirty to sixty minutes is a sensible study period.
- Regular study is better than occasional intensive study.
- Read the chapter through first to get an overview without doing any exercises. This will help you see what you want to focus on.
- Try the exercises before checking the Answer key.
- After doing the exercises in the book, try them again using your own research topic and reading materials. If possible, ask a more experienced colleague or friend to give you feedback on your work.
- All university departments are different. Use the information in the book as a guide to investigating your own university department.
- Write questions you can ask to find out how your department expects you to do research and collect and present data.
- There is no one correct way of doing research and working with collected data. Use your experience of doing the exercises to learn what works best for you. Adapt the suggestions in this book to suit your learning style and context.
- Learning to do research and work with data is an on-going process, which means you need to practise the same skills many times. Revise regularly.

Other titles

Also available in the *Collins Academic Skills Series: Writing, Lectures, Research, Presenting,* and *Group Work*.

1 | Getting started

Aims ✓ look at numbers in everyday life
✓ understand the purpose and use of statistics
✓ learn key terms for working with numbers
✓ learn the basics about spreadsheets
✓ practise referring to and labelling graphics in writing

Quiz
Self-evaluation

Read the statements below. Circle the answers that are true for you.

1	I understand what statistics is and the language to describe it.	agree	disagree	not sure
2	I know a number of basic terms and phrases to describe numbers in English.	agree	disagree	not sure
3	I know how to use a spreadsheet.	agree	disagree	not sure
4	I know how to refer to and label graphics such as bar charts and line graphs in writing.	agree	disagree	not sure

Glossary

data
You can refer to information as data, especially when it is in the form of facts or statistics that you can analyse. In American English, data is usually a plural noun. In technical or formal British English, data is sometimes a plural noun, but at other times, it is an uncountable noun.

Numbers and mathematics are very important in our everyday lives because we use them frequently when we manage our finances, go shopping, make travel plans, convert currency, follow instructions for a recipe or take measurements when we are building and creating things. If we carry out an academic study or investigation, then we need to use a branch of mathematics known as statistics which involves collecting and organizing data, making sense of our information and presenting findings.

This chapter begins by reminding us of the calculations and vocabulary that are used when we are working with money and taking measurements. It then provides an introduction to statistics, explaining where data is used in different subject areas and describing different categories of data. With a more technical focus, the chapter then describes how to use a computer program known as a spreadsheet which can help with storing and presenting data. Finally, an explanation is given of the use of graphics in academic writing, highlighting ways to refer to graphics in your text so that you can comment on your data and findings effectively.

Numbers in everyday life

In this section, we will explore some of the ways in which numbers are used in everyday situations. We will investigate taking measurements and working with money.

Money

It is important to know how to work with money so that you can:

- Recognize the value of amounts of money

- Estimate your expenditure

Often money calculations will involve the use of percentages and fractions. You will learn about these in Chapter 6.

The value of a digit in a number depends on its position in the number. In the following amounts of money, the digit 4 has a different meaning:

14p or £0.14	four pence
45¢ or 0.45¢	forty cents
£14.27	four pounds
$49.99	forty dollars
£458.60	four hundred pounds
€4,700	four thousand euros
$46,500	forty thousand dollars

A place value diagram may help to remind you how to recognize the value of amounts of money. The highest number in the group is the maximum and the lowest is the minimum.

$10,000	€1,000	£100	$10	£1	.	¢1/10	1/100p
ten thousand dollars	one thousand euros	one hundred pounds	ten dollars	one pound	.	ten cents	one pence

Estimating can be a useful skill when you are calculating your monthly expenditure because you can work out approximately how much your total bill will be without adding up all of the individual values. Estimating involves rounding prices up or down to the nearest ten pounds, dollars or euros so that you can work out the total more easily.

This list shows the actual expenditure with the estimated value for each cost:

Monthly Expenditure		
	Actual cost	Estimated cost
Accommodation	£512.40	£510
Food and drink	£148.60	£150
Travel	£31.52	£30
Clothes	£56.80	£60
Entertainment	£86.53	£90

So, when we add up the actual prices the aggregate total price for our shopping is £835.85 and the estimated cost is £840.

Measurements

Taking measurements is about finding a number that shows the amount or size of something. We are most often interested in measuring temperature, length, speed, time, capacity and mass. To make an accurate measurement, you would need to choose an appropriate measuring device and use the correct type of units on a scale. Here are some examples:

Measurement	Measuring device	Units
temperature	thermometer	degrees Celsius (°C) or degrees Fahrenheit (°F)
length	ruler or tape measure	centimetres (cm), metres (m) or kilometres (km)
speed	speedometer	metres per second (m/s) or kilometres per hour (km/h)
time	clock or stopwatch	seconds (sec), minutes (min) or hours (hr)
capacity	measuring jug	millilitres (ml) or litres (l)
mass	weighing scales	grams (g) or kilograms (kg)

Exercise 1

Match the correct unit of measurement with each item to be measured.

Unit of measurement	Item being measured
degrees Celsius (°C)	distance between London and Paris
kilometres (km)	weight of a pencil
kilometres per hour (km/h)	time taken to count to ten
seconds (sec)	temperature of a cup of coffee
millilitres (ml)	amount of orange juice in a glass
grams (g)	speed of a train

There are a number of key terms that are useful to learn when working with numbers and data. Test your knowledge of these by completing the following exercises.

Exercise 2

Use the words in the box to complete these sentences. You might need to change the form of the word.

accurate	calculation	fraction	measurement
aggregate / total	capacity	mass	percentage
approximately	estimated	maximum / minimum	round up / down

1   The _____ of 9, 10, 24, 6, 8, 5 is 62. It is also known as the _____.

2   The _____ of the lecture theatre is 200 people.

3   Economic forecasters have _____ that the economy will grow by 0.5% next year.

4   There are _____ 300,000 international students studying in the UK.

5   The spreadsheet automatically _____ or _____ to the nearest whole number.

6   The _____ loan available is £5,000 and the _____ loan available is £500.

7   The _____ of a bowling ball is 7.25 kilograms.

8   _____ measurements are essential in many scientific experiments.

Exercise 3

Use another word in the box in Exercise 2 to describe each item below.

1   1/3 _____
2   245 × 6 _____
3   98% _____
4   100 ml _____

Exercise 4

Put the word in brackets into the correct form in each of these sentences.

1   The closest _____ was 2 years 4 months. (estimate)
2   There are a number of different ways to _____ an average. (calculate)
3   There are _____ 1.3 billion people in China. (approximate)
4   The _____ of another variable completely changed the outcome of the experiment. (add)
5   The values were _____ and then used to find the average. (total)
6   The answers were cross-checked to _____ predict the outcome. (accurate)

What is statistics?

Glossary

method
A method is a particular way of doing something.

technique
A technique is a particular method of doing an activity, usually a method that involves practical skills.

Every day in our lives, we hear and read about many different types of information in the form of data. Data can tell us interesting and important details about the world around us but it can be challenging to understand the facts and figures.

Statistics is a mathematical science that helps us to make sense of data that has been counted, measured, asked about or observed. It involves four main activities:

Collecting data – first of all, we decide what type of data we are interested in, which method we shall use to collect the data, and where we would like to collect it from.

Glossary

feature
A feature of
something is an
interesting or
important part
or characteristic
of it.

Organizing data – we use a range of different techniques to summarize the data we have collected so that we can see interesting features or patterns in the information.

Interpreting data – we use the results of calculations to help us make comparisons about different sets of data, to answer questions and make decisions about the world around us.

Presenting data – when we have found out interesting facts about our data, then we will need to display and present the information to other people so that they can understand our conclusions.

Exercise 5

Choose a newspaper or news-related website and look for reports that use statistics to help explain the main points of the article. Think about these questions:

- How was the data collected?
- What type of organization is using the statistics?
- What interesting features or patterns were found in the data?
- How is the data presented?

Statistics is important in many different subject areas. The following diagram lists some examples of the type of data that might be collected and used:

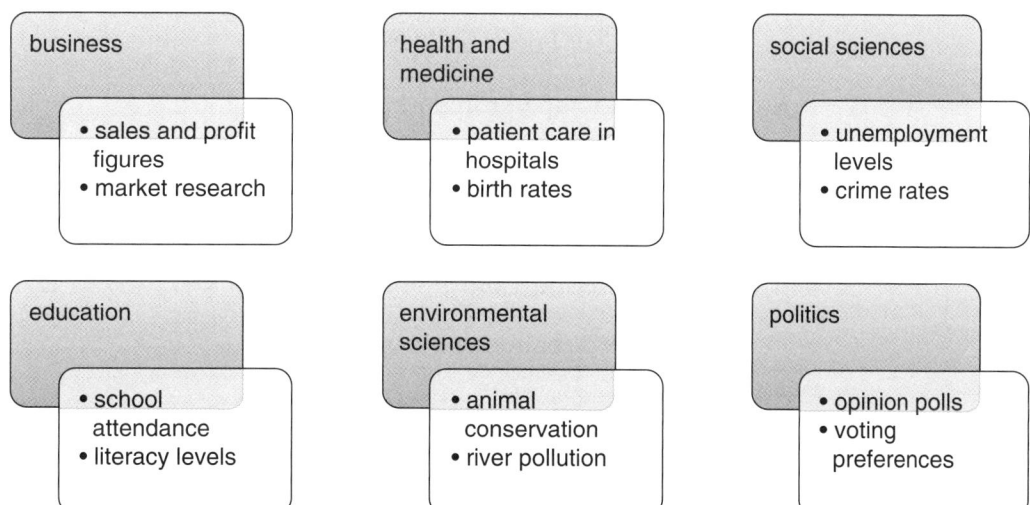

business
- sales and profit figures
- market research

health and medicine
- patient care in hospitals
- birth rates

social sciences
- unemployment levels
- crime rates

education
- school attendance
- literacy levels

environmental sciences
- animal conservation
- river pollution

politics
- opinion polls
- voting preferences

Some terminology

Glossary

variable
A variable is a factor that can change in quality, quantity, or size, which you have to take into account in a situation.

characteristic
The characteristics of a person or thing are the qualities or features that belong to them and make them recognizable.

attribute
An attribute is a quality or feature that someone or something has.

In statistics, we use two key words: variable and observation. It is important to understand the difference in their meanings. A variable is a characteristic or an attribute that can have different values; an observation is the value of a variable that has actually been counted, measured or observed. Some variables are shown below, with a list of possible observations next to each one.

Variable	Observations
favourite colour	purple, blue, orange
number of pets	3, 1, 0
time spent reading	2 hours, 1 hour
number of children in a family	1, 5, 2
eye colour	brown, blue
number of letters in a name	10, 4, 8

The observations for a variable can be described as **quantitative** or **qualitative**, depending on what the information is about. Quantitative data is something which can be measured or counted using a number. Qualitative data represents a characteristic that uses words to describe it but does not use any numbers.

Examples of quantitative variables are:

- time taken to complete a test

- the number of books in a library

- the highest temperature in a month

Examples of qualitative variables are:

- the nationality of people in a cinema

- the favourite sport of children in a school

- the colours of balloons at a party

Exercise 6

Match the words on the left to their definitions on the right.

1	A variable	a	Data which can be measured or counted using a number.
2	An observation	b	The value of a variable that has actually been counted, measured or observed.
3	Quantitative	c	Data representing a characteristic that uses words to describe it but does not use any numbers.
4	Qualitative	d	A characteristic or an attribute that can have different values.

Exercise 7

State whether each of the following variables is quantitative or qualitative:

1   number of pages in a book
2   names of students in a class
3   hair colour
4   weight of apples in a bag
5   height of trees in a park

Exercise 8

Answer these questions.

1   Explain the difference between a quantitative and a qualitative variable.
2   Give an example of each type of variable.
3   Explain why:

  'type of tree' is a qualitative variable

  'number of pupils in a class' is a quantitative variable

Exercise 9

Without looking back at the section 'What is statistics?', put these statistical stages into the correct order.

1   organize data

2   present data

3   collect data

4   interpret data

Exercise 10

Use the words in the box to complete these questions about the stages above.

data	features	patterns	sets of data
display	method	present	technique

1   What type of _____ are we interested in?

2   Which data collection _____ shall we use?

3   What _____ shall I use to summarize my data?

4   What interesting _____ or _____ can I see?

5   What questions do my _____ answer?

6   What is the clearest way to _____ and _____ my data?

Exercise 11

Match the questions in Exercise 10 to the stages in Exercise 9.

Using spreadsheets

You can store, organize and present your data in a computer program called a spreadsheet.

A spreadsheet appears as a table or grid containing a set of rows and columns. Rows are displayed horizontally on the grid and each one is labelled with a number (1, 2, 3 ...); the label for each column is a letter (A, B, C ...) and columns are displayed vertically across the grid.

The empty spreadsheet grid shown below has eight rows and five columns, but a spreadsheet in a computer program will have many, many more rows and columns.

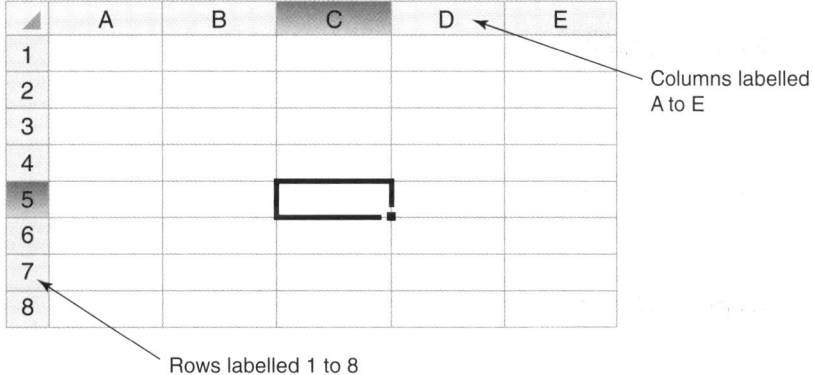

Columns labelled A to E

Rows labelled 1 to 8

The intersection of a row and a column is called a cell. Each cell has its own name, which consists of the letter of the column followed by the number of the row. The highlighted cell in the spreadsheet grid shown above is called C5 – it is where column C and row 5 meet.

Tip ✓ Use the glossaries to help you with some of the key words in this book. Consider making similar lists for your modules to help you learn key words.

Exercise 12

Look at the section of a spreadsheet below, and answer the questions.

	A	B
1	**Subject**	**Grade**
2	Statistics	80%
3	Information Systems	67%
4	Sociology	65%
5	Academic Skills	53%
6	Business and Management	74%

1   What is contained in the following cells?

   a   A6

   b   B3

2   What is the reference for the cells that contain the following?

   a   The number '53%'

   b   The word 'Statistics'

The data values in each spreadsheet cell can be displayed in different ways depending on how the information is described. You can use:

■   text

■   numbers

■   currency

■   dates and times

The spreadsheet opposite records the food purchased by a shopper at a supermarket. Row 1 in this grid is used to show the names of the columns so that it is easy to understand what information is being stored.

◢	A	B	C	D	E	F
1	**Item**	**Number purchased**	**Date purchased**	**Price**	**Total price**	
2	Toothpaste	2	15-Oct	£1.55	£3.10	
3	Orange	3	15-Oct	£0.25	£0.75	
4	Biscuits	1	15-Oct	£0.99	£0.99	
5	Bread	2	15-Oct	£1.35	£2.70	
6	Cheese	1	15-Oct	£1.54	£1.54	
7					**£9.08**	**Total**

Text   Number   Date   Currency

Glossary

formula
A formula is a group of letters, numbers or other symbols which represents a scientific or mathematical rule.

A spreadsheet is very useful for performing simple calculations. It uses formulae to perform operations such as addition, subtraction and multiplication.

The following spreadsheet shows the different nationalities of students enrolled on an English course. It includes a formula which uses the individual numbers of each nationality to calculate the total number of students enrolled on the course. The formula is usually hidden from view and only the result is displayed.

◢	A	B
1	**Nationality**	**Number of students**
2	Bahraini	7
3	British	9
4	Chinese	11
5	French	3
6	Kenyan	5
7	Japanese	2
8	Indian	6
9		
10	**Total**	**43**

The formula SUM(B2:B8) is used to calculate the total of number of students enrolled on the course. It adds up the numbers in cells B2 to B8. If a number in one of these cells is changed, then the result of the formula is automatically updated by the spreadsheet.

So, if another French student enrols on the course, then the cell B5 becomes 4 and the total in cell B10 is changed automatically to 44 to include the new student.

Once you have organized your data in a spreadsheet, it is then possible to use the computer program to create graphs and charts to display the information in a visual way. The bar chart below has been created using the data in the previous example.

For more information on graphics, see Chapter 8.

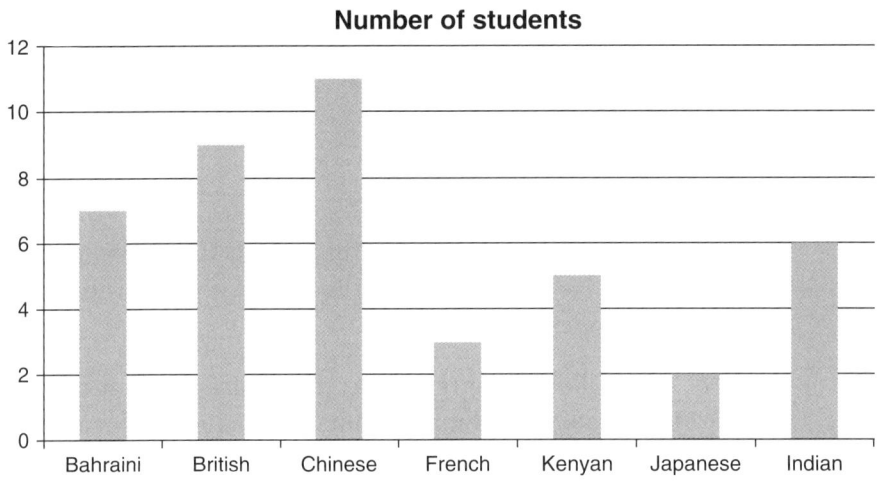

Number of students

Tip ✓ When using spreadsheets, you can click on the Help button in the computer program to search for advice on how to use formulae for calculations.

Using graphics

Glossary

proportion
A proportion of a group or an amount is a part of it.

trend
A trend is a change or development towards something new or different.

A number of different visuals are used in academic writing to present data or information. In academic texts they are often referred to as figures, but sometimes a wider range of terms such as *chart* and *table* are used as well. A **pie chart** is used to show the proportion of something in different segments. A key is used to label a pie chart when there are many sections. A **bar chart** is used to compare different amounts of something. A line graph is used to show trends or patterns. The axes are labelled to show what data is being presented. The x axis is horizontal and the y axis is vertical. A **table** is a grid with columns and rows of numbers. **Diagrams** are often used to describe functions. For example, they may show the organization of a company or the stages in the process involved in manufacturing or in decision-making.

Exercise 13

Look at the pictures below and label them with words from the box.

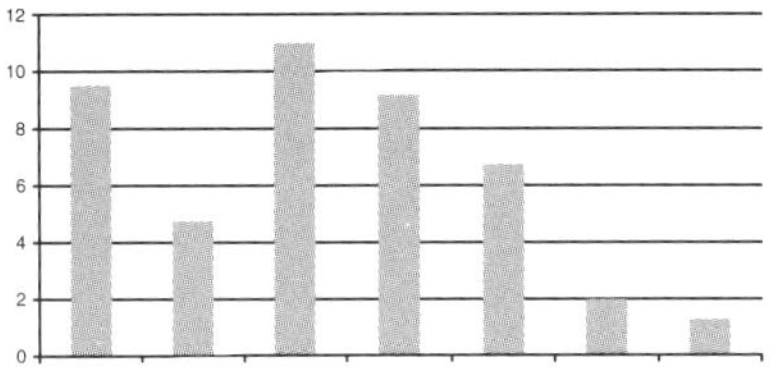

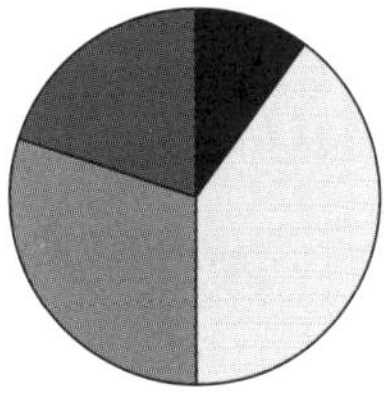

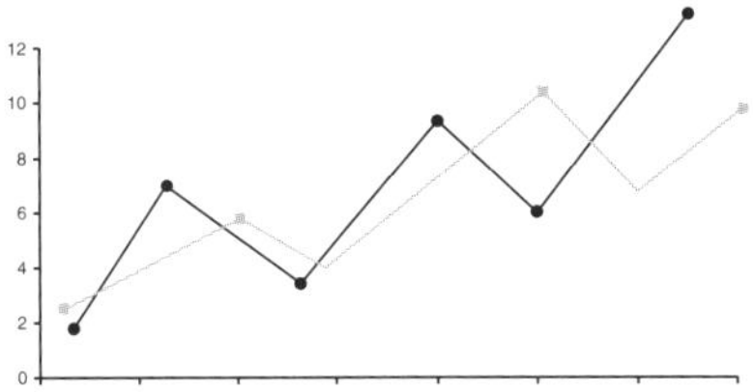

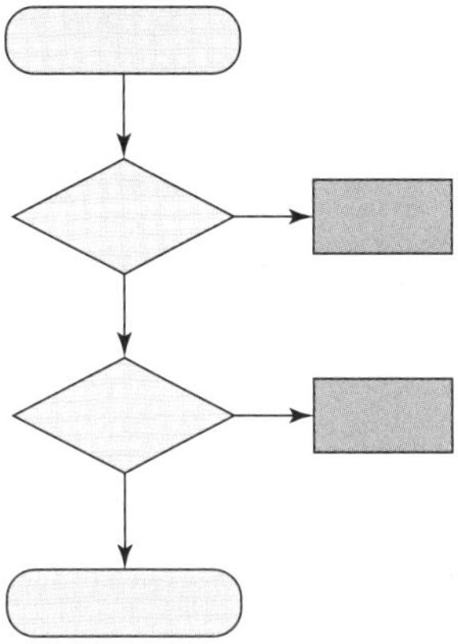

| Pie chart | Bar chart | Line graph | Table | Diagram |

Exercise 14

Put the words in brackets into the correct position and form in each sentence.

1 The x axis goes _____ and the y axis goes _____. (horizontal / vertical)

2 A _____ goes vertically and a _____ goes horizontally. (row / column)

3 A _____ is used to _____ a _____. With a _____ the _____ needs to be labelled. (label / key / pie chart / line graph / axis)

4 How many _____ are there in the _____ above? (segment / pie chart)

5 Graphics in academic writing are often referred to as _____ but sometimes as _____ or tables. (chart / figure)

6 Pie charts are generally used to show the _____ of something and line graphs to show _____. (trend / proportion)

Referring to graphics in writing

Although graphics generally speak for themselves, it is common to make a brief reference to them in writing to introduce what they show. This can be done with a range of basic phrases, for example:

As can be seen in Figure 12.1, …

From Table 2.1, it can be concluded that …

Language: relative clauses

Relative clauses can be a useful structure for summarizing or referring to key information in a graphic. For example:

- The graph shows the number of students from India *who were given visas in 2010* was 58,000.

- The table shows that the number of students *who come from the USA* is getting bigger.

In academic writing, relative clauses are often used for defining; in the case of data, they are used to describe or define exactly who or what you are referring to. Note that the relative pronoun (*who, whose, which, that*) will change depending on what you are defining. For people, use *who, that* or *whose* (possessive):

- The graph shows people *who are motivated by goals* often have short-term satisfaction.

- The graph shows that people *that set realistic goals* often enhance their performance.

- The chart demonstrates that companies *whose managers are not aware of employee motivation* are less likely to be successful.

For most things or ideas, use *that* or *which*:

- The table shows companies *that use money as a means to motivate employees*.

- The table shows teams *which use a sports psychologist to motivate teams*.

For more information on describing graphics, see Chapters 8 and 9.

Exercise 15

Complete the table with words from the box.

As is shown	graph 2.3	in	It can be seen from

As can be seen	from	Table 3.2,	...
It can be seen	2 _____	Figure 9.6	that ...
1 _____	in	3 _____	
According to			
4 _____			

Exercise 16

Match 1–5 with a–e to form sentences including a relative clause.

1	The charts shows that students are more likely to borrow a book	a	whose job is under threat are likely to be demotivated.
2	The table shows employees	b	who have both intrinsic and extrinsic motivation are more likely to succeed.
3	The chart shows people	c	which students find more challenging.
4	The chart shows areas of study	d	who receive praise outperform others.
5	The chart shows that workers	e	that is recommended by a course tutor.

Tip ✓ Try to record all new vocabulary in a similar way and regularly test yourself on the new words.

Remember

✓ You might have to use spreadsheets to analyse your data.

✓ The main purpose and use of statistics.

✓ Relative clauses are useful for referring to and labelling graphics in writing.

✓ The different stages from collection to presentation of data.

2 | Starting primary research

Aims ✓ practise formulating research questions

✓ understand the principles of sampling

✓ learn how to formulate a hypothesis

Quiz
Self-evaluation

Read the statements below. Circle the answers that are true for you.

1	I know how to start a primary research project.	agree | disagree | not sure
2	I know how to create an effective sample.	agree | disagree | not sure
3	I know which research method is most appropriate for my aims.	agree | disagree | not sure
4	I know how to formulate a hypothesis.	agree | disagree | not sure

Early planning and good organization are key to a successful research project. What you decide to research can vary greatly depending on the field you are in, but there are two main starting points: formulating research questions, or formulating a hypothesis to test. Whether you choose one, the other or both, there are some important points to consider:

- Does this area interest you enough? After all, this project will become a large part of your life for quite some time.

- Has this area been researched before? If so, what new things are you hoping to add with this study?

- How does this build on previous research in the area?

- Are the research aims focused and limited enough? You will have a limited amount of time and words to complete the project, so it needs to be realistic.

- Do you have access to a reasonable cross-section of the population you wish to study?

This chapter will help you to consider some of these key issues. It gives you practical steps to formulate research questions, and helps you understand the basic principles of sampling and to understand the cause and effect nature of hypotheses.

Formulating research questions

Doing a research project is both exciting and challenging at the same time. Research projects at the end of a Bachelor's or Master's (BA, BSc, MA, MSc) degree are commonly called a dissertation or a thesis. You usually have a lot of freedom to choose the area you want to research, although sometimes you may be given a choice of questions about a broad area of research to look into. You can start to think about the area you want to research very early on, but try not to narrow it down too soon before you are ready to begin.

It is a good idea to choose a topic or area that interests you, perhaps from a module you enjoyed or a topic that has stimulated your interest in a new area. Sometimes it can be a challenge to think of an area, so talk about it with tutors, friends or other students and perhaps look at some previous projects in your area of study.

Exercise 1

Follow these steps to help find an area that interests you.

1   Brainstorm the different subjects from your degree.

2   Think about particularly interesting modules.

3   Think of an interesting area from that module.

4   Which of these topics particularly interests you?

Once you have a range of topics that interest you, the next step is to narrow it down. This is something that should be done quite quickly as you often have limited time. Thinking about your motivation is important because you will be spending a lot of time on the project. It is also important to try to think about how practical the project is.

Being specific

One of the biggest challenges is choosing a research question that is specific enough. The idea of writing 15,000 or 20,000 words in your own language can make people feel quite worried, and doing it in another language for your Bachelor's or Master's degree can seem even more challenging. Many of the English exams to gain entry to a university only require students to write 250 words in English. So when, in perhaps just nine months of completing that test, you have to write 20,000 words, very few people worry about being specific. Many think – can I write that much? When people choose a topic that is too broad it can be difficult to answer in 15,000 to 20,000 words as there are too many things to cover. It can create problems conducting the literature review as you will have too many things to read. It could also mean that you do not have the time or resources to conduct your own research and write it up. Try to build on topics. Think about the following: has this area already been well researched? Is there a clear research methodology I could use? Can I bring a slightly new perspective to the topic? How specific you need to be will vary between courses, but it is essential you think about these questions in order to make your project realistic.

Exercise 2

Which of these research questions sounds specific enough?

1   Does regular exercise reduce stress levels in men aged 18–25?

2   Will a high-fibre and low-fat diet be sufficient to reduce cholesterol levels in middle-aged women?

3   Does exercise improve mental health?

4   Does motivation affect levels of effort?

Tip   ✓   Try to be as focused as you can from the start. Look at as many previous students' dissertations as possible to help guide you. Ask your supervisor for help and guidance when you feel you need it.

Exercise 3

Think about your possible research question and ask yourself these questions.

1   Can you answer your question in just a few months?

2   Is your question specific enough? Brainstorm all the different things you might include and then imagine how many words it might take to cover each.

3   Have you read previous students' projects? How long was each section?

4   Once you have collected your data how will you analyse it? How long do you think this might take? If you are doing something that requires you to write down what was said, for example an interview, practise this by recording a friend and writing down what they say. Time yourself and then imagine how long this might take once you have interviewed the number of people you want to interview.

5   Can you get access easily to people you want to interview, use in a focus group or give your questionnaire to?

Exercise 4

Decide if the following statements are true or false.

1	Being broad in your research aims is positive.	True / False
2	You shouldn't read previous students' work in case it's not very good.	True / False
3	Planning is key to a successful project.	True / False
4	Transcribing is quick and simple.	True / False
5	Finding a new angle on an existing topic is a good idea.	True / False

Sampling

Glossary

population
If you refer to a particular type of population in a country or area, you are referring to all the people or animals of that type there.

Population: when you carry out an investigation to find out information about a group of things or people, this group is known as the population.

Some examples of different populations are:

■   all the people who live in New York

■   all the books in a library

■   all the trees in a forest

■   all the nurses in a hospital

Census: you would need to carry out a census if you want to find out information about every member of a population. It is easier to carry out a census if you have a small number of people or things in your population, but if the population is very large then it is usually time-consuming, often expensive and sometimes impractical.

- For example, if a biscuit manufacturer that bakes thousands of biscuits every day decided to find out how easily their biscuits break, a census would involve breaking every biscuit that they make. This would be impractical because the population is too big and it would be very time-consuming to test each biscuit individually.

Sampling: instead of carrying out a census of the whole population, you could decide to ask questions or observe just a small group of the things or people within that population. This is called sampling. Using a sample can be a lot less expensive, quicker and much easier than carrying out a census. When you have collected information from a sample, it is then possible to draw conclusions and make estimates about the entire population.

- For example, the biscuit manufacturer in the previous example could use a sample to find out how easily their biscuits break by choosing 100 biscuits of different varieties for testing.

Exercise 5

For the investigations listed in the table below, describe the population and decide if it would be practical or impractical to carry out a census to find out information on the whole population.

Investigation	Sample population	Census: practical or impractical?
1 Finding out how many hours of homework are completed each week by the pupils in a specific class in a school.		
2 Finding out the number of pets that are owned by adults in London.		
3 Finding out the number of pages in each book in a large library.		
4 Finding out how many children in the UK walk to school in the morning.		

Avoiding bias

biased
If someone is biased, they prefer one group of people to another, and behave unfairly as a result. You can also say that a process or system is biased.

Using sample data, you can only draw conclusions and make estimates about the entire population if you choose a sample of things or people that represents the whole population fairly. If your sample is not representative of the population, then it is known as a biased sample.

The table below describes some samples taken for different investigations, and explains why these samples are not representative of the population. Can you work out why the sample is biased for the last two investigations?

Investigation	Sample	Why the sample is biased
The value of all houses in Bristol	Houses in one street in Bristol	Houses in the same street are likely to be similar in size, so the sample only fairly represents that street rather than all the houses in Bristol, which will vary considerably in size and therefore in value.
The favourite football team of men aged 20–40 in the UK	Men aged 20–40 who go to a football match between Manchester City and Manchester United in February	
People's opinion about whether driving a car is the best way to travel to work	Drivers who have just parked their car in a company car park	

Tip ✓ Ask someone else to look at your planned sample before you start your research and ask them if they can see any bias. It can be difficult to look at it objectively yourself, so help and guidance will be useful here.

Exercise 6

Match the words or phrases on the left to a definition on the right.

1	carry out	a	the group you want to investigate
2	investigation	b	a study of the whole group
3	population	c	to do a particular piece of work, research, etc.
4	census	d	not giving a fair representation of the entire population
5	sampling	e	typical of people or things in a particular group
6	draw a/the conclusion	f	the process of trying to discover all the details or facts about something to discover who or what caused it or how it happened
7	estimate	g	to say what you think an amount or value will be, based on the available information to calculate it
8	bias	h	to decide what to believe about something after you have considered the facts
9	representative	I	the process of selecting part of the whole population for your investigation

Exercise 7

Complete these sentences with words from Exercise 6. You may need to change the form of some words.

1 The sample was not large enough to be _____ of the whole population.

2 Poor _____ meant that it was difficult to draw conclusions.

3 The study was _____ over a three-month period.

4 The study aimed to _____ the effects of advertising on children.

5 The sample was _____ towards middle aged men.

6 The _____ net spend per month was £500.

7 A national _____ is carried out in the UK every few years.

8 The _____ under investigation was international students in the UK.

9 We can _____ the _____ that advertising has a significant impact on children's spending patterns.

Formulating a hypothesis

A hypothesis is something that you plan to test in your research and is related to forming your research question. The hypothesis usually states that something will or will not happen. It is something that you would write before starting your research; you plan to see if it is true or not after doing your research.

Examples of hypotheses:

- Language is the main challenge in adapting to another culture.

- Low income is the main reason for job dissatisfaction.

- Blueberries have a positive impact on the mind.

Each of these hypotheses is formed from two or more constructs and often makes a claim for cause and effect. For example:

Cause	Effect
language ability	ability to adapt to another culture
income level	job satisfaction
consumption of blueberries	impact on the mind

A construct is something that can be tested or questioned objectively. For example, in the first hypothesis above we could ask:

How can culture be defined?

How can adaptation be measured?

What factors affect adaptation?

How are language and culture related?

Does language impact on adaptation?

Exercise 8

What is the purpose of a hypothesis and what should it clearly state?

Exercise 9

Look at the other two hypotheses from the previous page. What questions could you ask yourself about these hypotheses?

Low income is the main reason for job dissatisfaction.

1   *How is job satisfaction defined?*

2   _____

3   _____

4   _____

5   _____

6   _____

Blueberries have a positive impact on the mind.

1   *What foods have a positive impact on the mind?*

2   _____

3   _____

4   _____

A piece of research may contain more than one hypothesis that will be tested. Another common thing other than cause and effect that is tested is a comparison between two groups or classes.

> **Example:**
>
> ■ Single sex schools produce better academic results than other schools. They are also more of an advantage for girls than boys.
>
> Here the hypothesis is looking at the cause and effect relationship between single sex schools and academic success but it is also making a comparison between boys and girls.

Exercise 10

Which of the following hypotheses make a comparison?

1 People who regularly use computers suffer from more health issues than those who do not use them.

2 Men make more impulse purchases than women.

3 It is more difficult to learn a second language after the age of 20 than before it.

4 Independent study increases academic success.

5 Three minutes' intensive exercise is enough to maintain fitness levels.

Exercise 11

Look at these possible causes and their effects. Can you join them together to write a hypothesis for each one?

1 Travel abroad > malaria

   Travelling abroad increases the risk of catching malaria.

2 Recycling > save money

3 Low temperatures > car accidents

4 Language learning > cultural awareness

Remember

✓ It is important to be specific in your research question.

✓ You need to define and clearly state your question early on in the research process.

✓ Sampling can have a significant impact on your research and should be done carefully.

✓ It is important to choose the most appropriate research methods.

✓ You can use hypotheses as part of your research process.

3 | Research methods

Aims ✓ understand some common research methods

✓ understand when to use interviews, questionnaires and focus groups

✓ understand the advantages and disadvantages of common research methods

Quiz
Self-evaluation

Read the statements below. Circle the answers that are true for you.

1	I know the difference between some of the more common research methods.	agree | disagree | not sure
2	I know when to use interviews, questionnaires and focus groups.	agree | disagree | not sure
3	I know how to construct an effective questionnaire and conduct a successful interview and focus group.	agree | disagree | not sure
4	I understand the advantages and disadvantages of some common research methods.	agree | disagree | not sure

A wide range of research methods is available for you to choose from when you conduct a research project. The key is to choose the most appropriate method or methods for your research aims. In Social Sciences, particularly with projects at undergraduate level, three of the most common methods are interviews, questionnaires and focus groups. This, of course, does not mean you need to limit yourself to these methods.

This chapter looks at some of the main research methods, at some of their main advantages and disadvantages and gives a brief overview of some other methods of research. The following two chapters look in more detail at how to produce a questionnaire and conduct an interview.

For more information on other research methods, see Further reading.

Choosing your research method

A research method is the way in which you choose to collect your data. A wide range of research methods can be used to gather data. This section will give you an overview before looking in more detail at some of the main advantages and disadvantages of four key research methods: questionnaires, focus groups, interviews and experiments. This is then followed by a brief overview of some other methods to consider. When you select your method it is important to choose one that will effectively help you to answer your research question or test your hypothesis. It is also important to be aware of the advantages and disadvantages of each method.

Questionnaires

Many students choose to do a survey using a questionnaire as it is commonly believed that the method is easy. A questionnaire doesn't involve the pressure of an interview, and the answers are conveniently written down for future analysis. However, it can be challenging to write an effective questionnaire.

Questionnaires can be distributed in a variety of ways and there is a varying amount of success in getting responses back. The questions are typically predominantly aimed at gathering quantitative data, but an element of qualitative data can also be gathered.

For more information on questionnaires, see Chapter 4.

Key considerations

Questionnaires are common in many people's everyday lives. Whether they are from a government department or a market research company, many of us will have answered a questionnaire in our daily life. This familiarity can mean that some people see questionnaires as the easy research option when in fact they are a challenging tool to use. There are some important things to remember when creating a questionnaire.

- The wording of questions is very important. Different people may understand words differently. For example, the words 'success' and 'satisfaction' can mean very different things to different people.

- Cultural background, age and social class can all affect people's understanding of questions.

- You need to be careful that all options have been presented and that any left out do not create biased results. It is also important not to lead people with your question to a particular answer. Ideally, the questionnaire should be piloted to help deal with these problems.

- Different respondents have variable memories, which can impact on the answers they give.

- Double questions, which often have *or* in the middle, are another thing to avoid when writing a questionnaire. For example: *When did you last buy your lunch or dinner in a restaurant?* If the answer is 'yesterday' we do not know if it was lunch or dinner or both that were eaten yesterday.

- It is not possible to tell when people are giving honest answers. People may give an answer that they think you want to hear or that makes them sound better. It is important to stress to the respondent the confidential nature of your questionnaire, but even then do not rely too much on these findings being accurate.

- Opinions are not stable and can change frequently, so it is important to remember that these results are only temporary.

- Other broader concerns you may have to consider are any difficulties or other challenges respondents may have in answering the questions, how simple the layout is and how consistently the questions are laid out.

Exercise 1

Decide whether the points below about questionnaires are advantages or disadvantages. Write A or D by each one.

1   They are easier to arrange than an interview. You simply need to distribute your questionnaire to your chosen sample.

2   Pre-coded questions are sometimes less demanding to answer, but respondents can find them frustrating to answer. The limited choice might mean that they cannot answer the question in the way they would like.

3   It is difficult for the researcher to check the truthfulness of an answer as they do not normally meet the respondent.

4   The answers are usually standard and therefore easy to analyse, although questionnaires do allow for some open questions which are harder to analyse.

5   It is quick and easy to collate the data compared to qualitative methods such as a focus group.

6   For respondents it can be easier and quicker to answer as the choices are limited.

7   Bias can be a problem as the options present the researcher's way of seeing things.

8   A large amount of data can be gathered for a limited amount of time and money.

9   The data can be more accurate when an internet-based survey is used. It can be designed so that the researcher does not need to enter the data.

Focus groups

Glossary

facilitate
To facilitate an action or process, especially one that you would like to happen, means to make it easier or more likely to happen.

Focus groups, or group interviews, are commonly used to gather qualitative data on thoughts, feelings and beliefs. They are common in the day-to-day work of companies and political parties. Typically, a focus group is formed of six to eight people, and multiple focus groups of around five or six people are common for a research project. The researcher facilitates the focus group by guiding topics.

Key considerations

One of the key considerations when choosing this as a research method is the skill it takes to effectively manage a focus group. Focus groups can have up to 20 participants but for inexperienced researchers it is probably best to limit the number to between six and eight. Around four, five or six groups will usually be enough groups for most research projects. People should be given name labels – these can be invented names if being

expression
The expression of ideas or feelings is the showing of them through words, actions or artistic activities.

attitude
Your attitude to something is the way that you think and feel about it, especially when this shows in the way you behave.

facilitator
A facilitator is a person or organization that helps another person or organization to do or to achieve a particular thing.

dominant
Someone or something that is dominant is more powerful, successful, influential or noticeable than other people or things.

anonymous is important. Using labels allows people to easily express agreement or disagreement with someone else.

At the start of the meeting it is important to explain how the focus group will work and how long it will last. Explain that it is important that all members are free to contribute equally. This can be important as it can help you manage a situation where one person dominates or other people say very little.

After you have introduced your topic your involvement should be as limited as possible. You shouldn't be a participant in the discussion, put forward your own views or comment critically on the discussion.

It can be useful to give participants a schedule to allow you to cover all of the topic areas you want people to discuss. Focus groups can be quite short, around 15 to 20 minutes or much longer depending on the topics and questions being discussed. It is important to have good quality audio equipment and you may even want to have an additional note-taker as it can be difficult to work out who is speaking on the recording.

Advantages

- Group participants are able to interact with each other. The group discussion can generate new thinking about a topic and lead to more in-depth discussion.

- The expressions, attitudes of individuals and the intensity of the conversation can be counted in the research result.

- People can be recruited based on certain criteria, e.g. sex, race and age.

- The facilitator has no control over the content, only the general topic.

- The facilitator can clarify certain points with the participants.

Disadvantages

- Focus groups can quickly become influenced by one or two dominant people.

- An inexperienced moderator may influence the discussion too much or allow people to dominate.

- Depending on the topic it can be difficult to have the participants share their real feelings towards something.

- Time and geographical constraints can make the method more unrepresentative than something like a questionnaire.

- The environment is quite unnatural, and the fact that people know they are being watched and recorded may affect the quality of research results.

Exercise 2

Listed below are some of the steps involved when you use a focus group to collect data. Decide which of the steps are taken **before, during** and **after** the meeting.

1   Give out name labels to participants.

2   Contact potential participants and invite them to the meeting.

3   Explain the purpose of the focus group and how long it will last.

4   Write a summary of the discussions and analyse your results.

5   Decide on the topic of your investigation.

6   Record the discussions using audio equipment.

7   Select participants who will be able to contribute ideas for your research.

8   Prepare the questions that you will ask to start a discussion.

Exercise 3

Describe two problems associated with collecting information using a focus group.

Interviews

Interviews involve asking a range of questions to individual people. They can be structured, semi-structured or unstructured. Structured interviews involve asking fixed questions that do not vary at all from one interview to the next. Semi-structured interviews cover fixed topics but allow some flexibility to explore a topic further if the respondent says something particularly interesting. Unstructured interviews do not have any pre-planned topics to cover. Interviews are a method perhaps most associated with qualitative data, but an element of quantitative data can be gathered, especially in a structured interview.

For more information on interviews, see Chapter 5.

For more information on qualitative and quantitative data, see Chapter 1.

Key considerations

In student-based projects the interviewer is nearly always the researcher. As a result, a lack of experience can often make people feel nervous when conducting an interview. Once you get used to interviewing, it will become much easier.

It is important to make sure your interviewee feels as comfortable as possible. You need to choose an environment where they can feel comfortable to answer your questions thoughtfully and with confidence. Try to avoid places with too many distractions and background noise.

The speed of the interview should largely be controlled by the interviewee's own style. Make sure the interviewee is free to offer additional information that could be of interest to your research. At the same time, try to maintain a steady pace. A successful interview won't feel very different from a normal conversation.

Make sure you follow any ethical considerations required in your institution. Also reassure the interviewee about the confidential nature of the interview.

In general the interviewer should limit their speaking time and allow the interviewee to dominate discussions. However, it is important for the interviewee to feel relaxed, so the amount the interviewer speaks will vary from person to person.

Advantages

- One of the main advantages of an interview is the depth of information collected. Topics can be discussed at length.

- Researchers already have conversational skills natural to a one-to-one discussion, meaning that fewer new skills, compared to managing a focus group, need to be learnt to make this method effective.

- The method puts the interviewee's opinions and ideas at the centre and gives them the chance to explain their thoughts.

- Interviewing is one of the most flexible methods of data collection. You can develop a line of enquiry while you are speaking.

- Interviews have a higher response rate than questionnaires.

Disadvantages

- Both the collection and analysis of the data can be time-consuming.

- Semi-structured and unstructured interviews mean the format is quite open and can make data analysis challenging.

- The effect the interviewer has on the situation can be strong. This can make the data less reliable.

- What people say, and what they do, do not always match. This can be especially influenced by the interviewer.

- The face-to-face nature and the recording equipment can make people nervous about speaking their mind.

For more information on interviews, see Chapter 5.

Experiments

Glossary

isolate
If you isolate something such as an idea or a problem, you separate it from others that it is connected with, so that you can concentrate on it or consider it on its own.

Key considerations

An experiment generally looks at cause and effect relationships. The aim is to control and isolate individual factors and to observe the effects. It is the method most typically linked with physical sciences but it is also used in social sciences. When establishing this relationship it is important to understand the difference between *independent variables* and *dependent variables*. An independent variable is something that exists and owes nothing to the other variables. An independent variable represents the **cause** of something, or the thing that explains why a situation happens, and can be tested to see if it is the cause of something. A dependent variable is the **effect** of something, and can be tested to see if it is the effect. It is the thing that changes as a result of the independent variable.

For example, the rate of obesity in the population would be the dependent variable and an independent variable might be the percentage of fat in diets. The researcher needs to know that it was this factor, the fat, and not another factor such as sugar or exercise that causes obesity.

The simplest way to do this is to introduce another variable and keep all other factors unchanged. The challenge is to make certain that the other variables remain unchanged. In some cases, rather than introducing a variable it can be easier to remove a variable. As with introducing another variable, the challenge is ensuring that other variables do not change.

Observation and measurement are key to experiments. In Social Sciences this can be a challenge as people may change their behaviour because they realize they are being observed. This is known as the 'observer effect' or the 'Hawthorne effect'. It is also important to pay attention to sampling and control groups when conducting experiments.

For more information on sampling, see Chapter 2.

Advantages

- One key advantage with an experiment is that if it is well recorded and the variables are controlled well, the experiment should be easy to repeat.

- Experiments have a high level of precision.

- Experiments can be conducted in the field but those that are conducted in the laboratory allow greater control over costs and time.

- For social scientists, experiments are given a high status as they are closest to the 'hard' sciences such as the natural sciences and computer science.

Disadvantages

- The use of control groups might affect how the experiment is carried out and bias the results. It also brings in ethical considerations.

- The setting is artificial and may not replicate the real world.

- It can be difficult to match the control group accurately to the experiment group.

- It can be challenging to control the different variables.

 **Exercise 4**

For each of the following pairs of variables, decide which variable is independent and which one is dependent.

Variable 1	Variable 2
amount of time spent on revision	score in a test
number of ice creams sold	temperature
number of colds suffered in a year	amount of fruit eaten each week
heart rate	running speed
plant height	amount of water given to a plant
price of laptop	number of laptops sold

 **Exercise 5**

Suggest an appropriate research method that you would use if you wanted to investigate the relationship between healthy eating and levels of fitness.

Further methods to consider

Observation

This method of data collection requires the researcher to observe people, animals or birds. It is typically used to gather qualitative data but data can be collected numerically as well. There are typically three methods of observation:

- participant observation

- covert observation

- non-participant observation

In participant observation the researcher lives or works with the subjects being studied. Covert observation is where the researcher's identity is not revealed. Ethical considerations mean it is often difficult to conduct such research. Non-participant observation is where the

Glossary

archive
The archive or archives are a collection of documents and records that contain historical information. You can also use archives to refer to the place where archives are stored.

journal
A journal is an account which you write of your daily activities.

reflection
Reflection is careful thought about a particular subject. Your reflections are your thoughts about a particular subject.

researcher is 'outside' the group but looking on. All methods typically look at behaviour, interaction and language.

Analysis of written or spoken language

This method looks at analysing spoken or written records. It is common in subjects such as History and Linguistics. Three methods typically used are:

- content analysis

- thematic analysis

- linguistic analysis

Content analysis might look at written materials such as diaries, archives, film scripts or newspaper articles. Thematic analysis studies the social meaning of written or spoken language. Linguistic analysis looks at how people use language and how it is used in a particular situation.

Secondary analysis of data

One method of research can be the re-analysis of data already collected. The data can be gathered from resources such as government statistics or research conducted by specific research companies. It can also be data provided by a teacher or researcher. The re-analysis can produce fresh perspectives on an issue or mean that it can be looked at for something different, such as geographical variations for example.

Action research

Action research is used within a variety of settings in the Social Sciences, and is used in particular in the fields of education, organizational development, health and social care. Action research is involved in practical issues, problems and concerns that occur in the real world. The researcher is very much involved in the setting that is being studied, for example, a teacher researching an issue in their own classroom. It is used to gain a better understanding of everyday issues and often to then make changes to deal with the issue or problem. The technique involves observations, journals and reflections in order to identify the problem and/or issue and the best method of dealing with it. The application of the findings is part of the research process. The researcher is very active in the process and the nature of the research is cyclical.

Case studies

Case studies focus on one or just a few instances of a situation. They look in depth at events, relationships and experiences. A case study looks at things in great detail, usually in a natural setting, in other words one that is not created for the purposes of research. A variety of research methods can be used, including observation, interviews and questionnaires. A case study can be based on things such as individuals, organizations or policies.

Exercise 6

For each of the following situations, decide whether the data should be collected using an experiment, an observation or a questionnaire.

1   An investigation into the feeding habits of birds of prey.

2   Research about the use of computer games among teenage boys.

3   A study of how families spend their summer vacation time.

4   An investigation into how well women over 50 can remember a sequence of four-letter words.

See Further reading for more details on these research methods.

Remember

✓   A wide variety of research methods is available and some will be more appropriate to your situation than others.

✓   In Social Sciences at undergraduate level, interviews, questionnaires and focus groups are perhaps the most common research methods, but other methods such as action research can be used.

✓   The advantages and disadvantages of each method.

4 | Questionnaires

Aims
- ✓ understand how to write a questionnaire
- ✓ practise forming polite questions
- ✓ understand different sampling techniques
- ✓ understand the pros and cons of distribution methods

? Quiz
Self-evaluation

Read the statements below. Circle the answers that are true for you.

1	I understand what good and bad questions are in a questionnaire.	agree | disagree | not sure
2	I know how to form polite questions.	agree | disagree | not sure
3	I know how to use different sampling methods.	agree | disagree | not sure
4	I know how to distribute a questionnaire effectively.	agree | disagree | not sure

Questionnaires are a popular research tool for many undergraduates in their social science research project. There is often the perception that they are easy to write, easy to distribute and easy to analyse. However, it can be challenging to write a questionnaire as there are many simple mistakes that will impact on the quality of the data you collect. Being clear and consistent in your wording will also impact on the responses you get.

Questionnaires cannot, in general, simply be distributed to anyone, and the sample needs to be considered carefully. In this chapter we will look at a number of different sampling methods and then look at the different methods of distribution and the pros and cons of each method.

Writing a questionnaire

Questionnaires are usually made up of questions that require responses that produce qualitative data. The main difference here is between closed and open questions. Open questions are ones that allow people to write or say anything in response to a question. For example:

How do you feel about children starting school at the age of four?

Open questions usually gather more full answers as respondents can say what they want. However, too many open questions might make a respondent less willing to answer your questionnaire as they take more time and effort to answer. More time is required to analyse the responses to open questions before the data can be used.

Closed questions allow a more limited variety of responses. They can be simple yes/no questions, use a scale or offer a range of choices. For example:

- *Is four the right age for children to start school?*

- *Children should start school at the age of four.*

| Strongly agree | Agree | Neutral | Disagree | Strongly disagree |

- *Which of the following is the best age for a child to start school?*

| 4 | 5 | 6 | 7 |

The main advantage of closed questions is that they allow for simple analysis because the data is quantitative. However, there is less chance for the respondent to give the exact answer that they want. For example, to the question *Is four the right age for children to start school?* they might think it is fine depending on a number of factors such as maturity, gender, language ability, etc. However, the question does not allow them to express this opinion. Due to this, respondents might get frustrated with closed questions as they feel they cannot say exactly what they want to say.

Exercise 1

Look at the questions below. Which ones are open and which are closed?

1   Do you think children should finish school at 18?

2   Are you happy with your child's school?

3   What are the positives about your child's school?

4   How much homework is your child given?

5   Do you think your child is given enough homework?

6   What do you think are the benefits of going to university?

The following are some common ways of forming questions for a questionnaire.

An open question
What do you think about India's education system?

A yes/no answer
Have you studied in another country? Yes / No

Agree/disagree statements
Would you agree with the following statement?
Experience is more important than education.

Choose from a list of options
Which ONE of these is the most attractive holiday destination?

China	Mexico	Russia	Sweden	Thailand
the UAE	the USA	Tunisia		

Rank order
From the following list of European countries choose the THREE which you feel are the most economically successful. Rank them in order.
Italy, the UK, Ireland, Greece, Poland, Spain, Hungary, Norway

Likert scale

The break-up of the European Union will help all countries.

| Strongly agree | Agree | Neutral | Disagree | Strongly disagree |

Rate items

How significant would you rate the following factors in learning a language?

	Not significant						Significant
Motivation	1	2	3	4	5	6	7
Age	1	2	3	4	5	6	7
Intelligence	1	2	3	4	5	6	7
Aptitude	1	2	3	4	5	6	7

Common mistakes

There are a number of mistakes that people often make when writing questions for a questionnaire. Some questions are double barrelled, i.e. within one question people are in fact asked to respond to two questions, to which different responses are possible.

Examples:

Incorrect:

Please indicate how much you agree or disagree with each of the following statements about the hotel.

The room was comfortable and clean.

If a person thinks the room was comfortable but not clean, then putting them together in one statement makes it almost impossible to answer.

Correction:

Please indicate how much you agree or disagree with each of the following statements about the hotel.

The room was comfortable.

The room was clean.

Glossary

overlap
If one idea or activity overlaps with another, they involve some of the same subjects, people, or periods of time.

Some questions can be biased, or leading, and push the respondent to give you the answer you want to hear. For example:

Incorrect:

How much will prices go up next year?

Correction:

What will happen to prices next year?

There can also be an overlap between some categories. For example:

Incorrect:

Did you first hear about the election result:

_____ *from a friend or relative?*   _____ *from your partner?*

_____ *from a newspaper?*   _____ *at work?*

_____ *from the television or radio or other electronic media?*

Correction:

Did you first hear about the election result:

_____ *from a friend?*

_____ *from a relative?*

_____ *from a media source?*

Sometimes not enough categories are given. For example:

Incorrect:

At what level did you finish your education?

High School _____   *Bachelor's Degree (BA/BSc)* _____
Master's Degree (MA/MSc) _____

Correction:

At what level did you finish your education?

High School _____   *Bachelor's Degree (BA/BSc)* _____
Diploma _____   *Master's Degree (MA/MSc)* _____
Doctorate (PhD) _____

Exercise 2

Look at the following questions and try to improve them.

1   *Citizen Kane* is often rated one of the best movies ever. Have you seen this movie?

    Yes   No

2   In your opinion, how would you rate the speed and quality of your work?

    Excellent   Very good   Good   Fair   Poor

3   What do you think is your biggest expense every month?

    _____ rent   _____ travel   _____ childcare

4   Where do you get most or all of your information about health?

    _____ doctors   _____ internet   _____ friends   _____ books

Tip ✓ It is important to pilot any research method you plan to use. To pilot something means that you test it out on individuals or groups of people and then make changes based on any weaknesses you observe.

Forming polite questions

It is important to create a good impression when you first approach someone. They are more likely to agree to answer your questionnaire or take part in your interview if you are polite and friendly. One simple technique is to use indirect questions when you first approach someone. This can be done with the use of phrases.

Examples:

- Would you mind ...?

- Could you ...?

- Can I ...?

- I'd like to ...?

- I was wondering if ...?

For example:

- *How old are you? > Would you mind telling me how old you are?*

Notice the change in word order with direct and indirect questions in *How old are you?*

Exercise 3

Put the following words in the correct order to make polite questions.

1   you / spare / a few moments / could?

2   mind / would / you / taking / in my survey / part?

3   I / ask / could / old / how / are /you?

4   was / if you / had / time to / I / wondering / a / questions / few / answer?

5   I / ask / what / your / can / is / profession?

6   I'd like / to / ask / take / a few minutes / some questions / you / if possible?

Selecting your sample

Glossary

generalized
Generalized means involving many different things rather than one or two specific things.

random
A random sample or method is one in which all the people or things involved have an equal chance of being chosen.

In Chapter 2, we made a distinction between a population and a sample, noting that collecting data using a sample can be a lot less expensive, quicker and much easier than carrying out a census. The main aim in selecting your sample should be to ensure as far as possible that the sample is representative of the entire population, so that any observations made about the sample can be generalized to the population.

There are several different methods that you could use to choose your sample – random, opportunity, quota and cluster techniques.

Random sampling

In random sampling, each member of the population has an equal chance of being selected to be part of the sample. There are three basic steps to creating a random sample:

Step 1 – Starting 1, 2, 3, give a unique number to each person, i.e. each member of the population is given a different number.

Glossary

quota
A quota is the limited number or quantity of something which is officially allowed.

cluster
A cluster of people or things is a small group of them close together.

discrete
Discrete ideas or things are separate and distinct from each other.

Step 2 – Use a computer or a calculator to generate a set of random numbers.

Step 3 – Create your sample by choosing the members of the population whose numbers match the set of random numbers.

Opportunity sampling

To use an opportunity sampling method, you simply ask people who are willing or available to fill in your questionnaire or be interviewed. This sample is not likely to be representative of a larger population because it will probably involve people in the local area or friends, family and colleagues of the researcher. For example, if you decided to choose your sample from people leaving a specific shop on a Tuesday morning, then only the people present in that place and at that time would be able to take part in the investigation.

Quota sampling

Quota sampling is a useful technique if the population being considered is naturally made up of several groups or categories which contain people with similar characteristics, for example: age, gender, marital status or job type. In this case, you would choose to include in your sample a certain number of people from each group. For example, from the population of students in a school, you might decide to choose five girls and five boys from each class.

Cluster sampling

In cluster sampling, you divide your population into discrete geographical areas, known as clusters. Choosing a random sample of clusters, you then include all of the people in each cluster in the sample. For example, if you are interested in the income of households in a particular area of Shanghai, you might choose to carry out a survey of every household in ten randomly chosen streets. This method will create an unbiased sample if the people within the chosen clusters are representative of the entire population.

To help you choose the most appropriate sampling method for your investigation, the following table summarizes some of the advantages and disadvantages of the different sampling techniques.

Sample method	Advantages	Disadvantages
Random	A random sample is completely unbiased because every member of the population has an equal chance of being chosen.	It is not an effective sampling method to use when you are not able to list all of the members of the population.
Opportunity	Opportunity sampling can be carried out quickly and inexpensively.	Usually these samples are biased because the people chosen for your sample are only the ones who are available at that time and place.
Quota	If you are not able to list all of the members of the population, then this can be a useful method.	Quota sampling can be biased because the researcher chooses the members of the population to be included in the sample from each group.
Cluster	This is a convenient method which reduces travel time if the population is spread over a wide area.	The results can often be biased because people living or working in the same geographical area probably have similar characteristics.

Exercise 4

Explain the main differences between opportunity sampling and quota sampling.

Exercise 5

Describe an investigation for which it would be appropriate to use random sampling to select your sample of people from the entire population.

Exercise 6

Decide if the following investigations involve cluster, quota or opportunity sampling:

1 In a survey about holiday destinations, a researcher goes to an airport and interviews 20 men travelling alone, 20 women travelling alone, 20 couples without children and 20 couples with children.

2 An investigation into how much money people spend on eating out involves distributing a questionnaire to all of the diners in a restaurant on a Saturday evening between 7 pm and 9 pm.

3 When researching people's attitudes towards recycling, a random sample of ten streets is chosen and then each household in those streets is asked about their recycling habits.

Distribution methods

When you have designed the questions for your survey and chosen the people who will make up your sample, you should then consider how you will distribute the questions to people and how you will collect their responses.

You could use one of the following methods to distribute your questionnaire:

Send it in the post
- You will be able to reach a wide geographical area.
- The postage costs can be expensive.
- You cannot be sure which member of a household will answer the questions.

Hand it out yourself
- You will be able to give the survey directly to the people in your sample.
- This method can be very time-consuming.
- Some people may not like to be approached directly.

People can choose to take one
- You might use this method for a customer satisfaction survey.
- The answers might be biased because only people who have had a very good experience or a very poor experience might choose to take one.

Online distribution

Alternatively, you could decide to create an online questionnaire to be distributed and returned electronically using a computer.

Using an online system has several advantages. It will reduce the costs and time taken for distribution and collection because there is no printing or posting involved in this method. You can also use a computer to create a survey that looks more interesting and uses features such as pop-up images and drop-down menus to encourage people to take part. The responses received for an online questionnaire can be processed electronically by being input directly into a spreadsheet or other type of computer program.

However, there are also some problems associated with online questionnaires. It is more likely that someone receiving the survey electronically will delete the email compared to throwing away a paper copy that arrives in the post. Also, from the researcher's point of view, creating an online survey can be much more time-consuming than producing a paper version because it will be necessary to use a specialist software program. Even though an online questionnaire may be successfully received by a person, technical problems may mean that they are unable to answer the questions or return it to you.

Exercise 7

Describe two advantages and two disadvantages of using online questionnaires rather than distributing them by post.

Non-response

Glossary

incentive
If something is an incentive to do something, it encourages you to do it.

Often researchers find that very few people in their sample decide to return a completed survey. There can be many reasons for a low response rate, but it is usually because people do not have time or are not interested in the investigation. There are a few ways in which you can encourage people to take part in the investigation:

- Use the start of your survey to tell people about the investigation; interest them in the subject area and explain what the data will be used for.

- Make sure your questions are clear and easy to answer to reduce the time it takes to complete them all.

- Make suitable arrangements to collect the completed questionnaires yourself so that people will have a deadline to aim for.

- Offer an incentive to people who respond; this could be entry to a prize draw, discount vouchers or free advice.

Pilot studies

A pilot study is usually used to test the quality of the questions in your survey. It involves asking a small group of people, often friends or family members, to fill out the survey and give their opinion on the questions. It should help you find any questions that are difficult for people to understand or ones that they are reluctant to answer. It is useful to keep a record of the pilot study results and the changes you make to your survey as a result of the feedback.

Exercise 8

You decide to carry out an investigation to find out about the types of books that are read by students on a university campus. Describe two different types of incentive you could offer to maximize the number of students who are willing to fill in a questionnaire.

Exercise 9

Explain the best way to test the quality of the questions in your survey before you distribute it to all of the people in your sample.

Remember

✓ Questionnaires are often thought of as quite simple but it is actually quite difficult to write an effective one.

✓ It can be important to use polite question forms when asking for information.

✓ The sampling technique you use will have a large impact on the data you collect.

✓ There are many pros and cons of different questionnaire distribution methods.

5 | Interviews

Aims
- ✓ understand how to ask good interview questions
- ✓ learn how to structure different questions
- ✓ learn about the interviewer effect
- ✓ learn how to use reported speech

? Quiz
Self-evaluation

Read the statements below. Circle the answers that are true for you.

1	I understand what makes a good interview question.	agree | disagree | not sure
2	I know how to structure different questions.	agree | disagree | not sure
3	I know what bias is and how to avoid it.	agree | disagree | not sure
4	I know how to use reported speech.	agree | disagree | not sure

Interviews are one of the most common research tools in the Social Sciences. They allow for a topic or topics to be discussed in great detail with a small group of respondents. Often time and finances do not allow for a large number of interviews to be conducted on a student project. Due to the fact that interviews can at first feel like a simple conversation, there can be the belief that they are an easy research tool. However, there are a number of challenges that can impact on the quality of the data collected.

In this chapter we will look at a number of topics that will help you to conduct an effective interview. Firstly, we will look at how to write a range of different questions depending on the data you want to collect. The chapter will then discuss how to write and structure different question types. Who the interviewer is and how they conduct the interview can also have an impact on the data collected, and we will take a brief look at some of the related issues. Finally, the last section will look at reported speech as one structure you can use to discuss your findings.

Good interview questions

One of the most important things to remember when using interviews as your research method is that interviewees should feel free to answer in their own words. It is important to create an environment where the respondent feels relaxed. Planning, preparing and piloting will help you to learn how to create such an environment.

Interview questions can be simple or quite complicated and they tend to cover five main areas. However, they can broadly be divided into different categories – **Facts and knowledge, Opinions and beliefs** and **Feelings.** Below are some examples of the different question types.

General facts

- *How old are you?*
- *How much money do you spend on food each week?*
- *What make of mobile phone do you have?*

Facts about past events

- *How often did you eat out last month?*
- *When did you start your current job?*
- *Have you ever travelled to Latin America?*

Interviewee knowledge

- *Do you know the name of the Egyptian president?*
- *Do you know anyone who shops in Tesco?*
- *Which countries founded the European Union?*

Opinions and beliefs

- *Do you think that the economic situation will improve next year?*
- *Do you believe in euthanasia?*
- *Do you agree or disagree with this statement? 'People make their own luck.'*

Feelings

- *Did you have a close relationship with your parents?*
- *How do you react when under pressure?*
- *How do you feel when people comment on your work?*

Exercise 1

Look at the questions below and decide which question type they are.

1 Who was the newest member of the EU?

2 How often did you go to the cinema last year?

3 Would you say that people in the financial sector earn
a too little?   b a fair salary?   c too much?

4 When were you born?

5 What is the speed limit in your country?

6 How do you feel when you have to speak in public?

7 Do you think online gambling should be banned?

8 Have you ever been scuba-diving?

Exercise 2

What question could you ask to find the answer in each of these situations?

1 You want to find out how someone feels about their relationship with their siblings.

2 You want to know someone's opinion about happiness.

3 You want to know how someone feels about brands.

4 You want to know where someone lives.

5 You want to know which of these someone values more:

fame	happiness	health	wealth

6 You want to know if someone knows who the leader of the UN is.

7 You want to know where someone went on holiday last year.

8 You want to know what someone believes is the role of charities.

Structuring questions

auxiliary verb
An auxiliary verb is a verb which is used with a main verb, for example to form different tenses or to make the verb passive.
In English, the basic auxiliary verbs are 'be', 'have', and 'do'. Modal verbs such as 'can' and 'will' are also sometimes called auxiliary verbs.

Yes/no questions

In Chapter 4 we looked at polite question forms and open and closed questions. One of the simplest closed questions is a yes/no question. They are formed by beginning with an auxiliary verb. An auxiliary verb is a form of *be*, *have* or *do* or a form of a modal verb, e.g. *can*, *will*. The auxiliary comes before the subject.

Auxiliary	Subject	
Have	you	got a tablet?
Can/Could	you	find the product?
Are/Were	you	working?
Do/Did	you	run every day?
Will/Would	she	change her mind?

If there is more than one auxiliary, only one comes before the subject:

***Could** you have done better?*   ***Have** you been on holiday this year?*

Note that the auxiliary verbs *be*, *have* and *do* can also be the main verb in the sentence.

Exercise 3

What would you say in each of these situations?

1   You want to know if the respondent has played games online.

    Have you played games online?

2   You want to know if the respondent would shop online again.

3   You want to know if the respondent enjoyed their stay in the hotel.

4   You want to know if the respondent ever travels to work by train.

5   You want to know if the respondent has ever been camping.

6   You want to know if the respondent is free to answer some questions.

7   You want to know if the respondent does exercise every day.

Wh-questions

Most *wh*-questions begin with the question word, followed by an auxiliary and then the subject.

Question word	Auxiliary	Subject
Why	have	you changed internet service provider?
What	is	your opinion of the show's new format?
When	did	you last shop online?
Where	are	you planning to go on holiday next year?
How	could	working conditions be improved?
Who	was	your inspiration as a child?

Exercise 4

Complete the questions to these answers.

1	_____ the prime minister of the UK in the year 2000?	Tony Blair.
2	_____ the Olympic games held?	Every four years.
3	_____ you feel when you got the news?	I felt delighted.
4	_____ you think about the government cuts?	I don't agree with them.
5	_____ you go to university?	In Los Angeles.
6	_____ you spend on the internet every day?	About three hours.
7	_____ you visit family members?	Usually once a month.
8	_____ you spend on your last phone?	£250.

Subject/object questions

Questions can be structured to ask about a subject or object. For example:

Subject questions:

What will happen next? (something will happen next)

Object questions:

What will they do next? (they will do something next)

Exercise 5

Look at the questions below and decide which ones are subject questions and which are object questions.

1   How many people did you speak to?

2   What did you learn?

3   What is worrying you?

4   Who would be best to lead the country?

5   How long did you spend on the task?

6   Which program will work best?

Prepositions in *wh*-questions

In *wh*-questions the question word is the object of a preposition, for example, *for* or *about*.

What do you worry about most?

What do you use the internet for?

A question with *what … for* is usually concerned with finding out about purpose. We can also use the combination *what … like* to find out about people's feelings or opinions on a topic.

What is the United Nations for?

What has your experience of the UK been like?

Exercise 6

Put the words below into the correct order to form questions.

1   choose / what / did / you / that / for / course?

2   what / of / holidays / kind / of / interested / in / are / you?

3   countries / lived / which / have / in / you?

4   the / weather / what's / where / live / you / like?

5   most / commonly / what / you / do / complain / about?

6   live / with / who / do / you?

The interviewer effect

We have already looked at bias in Chapter 2 in terms of making sure the sample you select is not biased. However, bias is an issue that needs attention at all stages of the research process. In terms of actually conducting the interview, bias can be created by what is often known as the interviewer effect. An interviewee is likely to respond differently depending on how they perceive the interviewer. In other words, their answers can change depending on who the person interviewing them is. For example, the sex, age, ethnic origin, qualifications, profession and social status of the interviewer can have an impact on the amount and type of information the interviewee is likely to give. Some studies have found that the same questions will generate different answers depending on who the interviewer is. For example, a study on race-related issues found that some questions would get less liberal responses if the interviewer was African-American than if the interviewer was white. It is harder to judge the impact of social status as it includes many factors such as education, profession and income. However, if a survey is being conducted on a topic such as beliefs about success, respondents might differ in their response if the interviewer is seen to be more or less successful in areas such as education, wealth or their profession.

There are limits as to what can be done to avoid the impact of this in a small-scale research project, but using the internet or the phone can to some extent hide who we are. Obviously, in general we cannot hide certain personal attributes such as our sex, accent or profession, but we need to consider how these factors might influence the data we collect.

Exercise 7

Look at the questions below and think about how they might impact on the data collected for your own research project.

1   How might an age gap affect the data collected?

2   Does the topic being researched mean that interviewing someone of the opposite sex or from a different ethnic background will affect the interview?

3   What are the qualifications, profession and social status of the person being interviewed? How do they compare to my own and what might the impact be?

Reported speech

Glossary

aspect
Aspect is the way that a verb group shows whether an activity is continuing, is repeated, or is completed. For example, in 'They were laughing', the verb is in the progressive aspect and shows that the action was continuing.

When learning about reported speech in a general English course, there is often a tendency to focus on changing the tense of the verb, for example, changing the present simple to the past simple. However, in academic writing, having a good knowledge of tenses is less of a concern. In academic writing, the simple aspect is used most often. The perfect and continuous aspect are more common in news and literature. Furthermore, most verb forms take the past or present simple and there are fewer verbs than nouns in academic writing. For example:

If the project fails we have no chance of becoming market leader.

Conversation has a high density of verbs and the verb to noun ratio is roughly equal. However, in academic writing the ratio of nouns to verbs is very different. For example:

A relative share of 0.8 means that the product achieves 80 per cent of the market leader's sales volume (or value).

In academic writing there is a high density of nouns and the verb to noun ratio is roughly 1 to 4.

Consequently, the most useful reporting structure to learn is *verb + that* and then to decide whether to use the present or past simple. If something is considered true regardless of time then use the present simple; this is more likely to be the case when talking about secondary research rather than primary research. If you are reporting past research or opinions then use the past simple; this is more likely to be the form you will use for secondary research.

According to a study by Durrant (2009), the most common verbs used in this reporting structure are:

argue, assume, conclude, confirm, demonstrate, emphasize, hypothesize, imply, indicate, note, predict, reveal, show, speculate, suggest, suppose

Learning the different meanings of these words and how to use this pattern will help you to write up a report of your findings.

Exercise 8

Below are some of the most common reporting verbs used with *that*. Match the verbs to their definition.

1	argue	a	to decide by reasoning; deduce
2	assume	b	to show or prove, especially by reasoning or evidence, etc.
3	conclude	c	often followed by *for* or *against* to present supporting or opposing reasons or cases in a dispute; to reason
4	confirm	d	to stress the importance of something
5	demonstrate	e	to prove to be true or valid; corroborate; verify
6	emphasize	f	to suggest an explanation for a group of facts or phenomena, either accepted as a basis for further checking or accepted as likely to be true
7	hypothesize	h	to take for granted; accept without proof; suppose
8	imply	i	to express or indicate by a hint; indirectly suggest

Exercise 9

Use the words in italics next to each sentence to complete each gap with a word from the box. You may need to change the form of the verb.

indicate	note	predict	reveal	show	~~speculate~~	suppose

1 Researchers have __*speculated*__ that population growth may not continue. *guessed*

2 Initial studies _____ that blueberries have a positive impact on memory. *give a sign*

3 The results _____ that education is a good predictor for future economic success. *present/prove*

4 Johnson _____ that further research is needed. *makes particular mention of*

5 Many people _____ that the European Union will collapse. *make a declaration about the future*

6 The study _____ that people's perceptions have changed. *expose something hidden*

7 The theory _____ that GDP growth is positive. *assumes*

Exercise 10

How would you report these findings?

1 A study that wants stricter controls on labelling of food packaging.

Johnson and Smith (2010) …

Johnson and Smith (2010) argue that stricter controls are needed on food labelling.

2 A study that forecasts the decline of fish stocks.

The organization …

3 A study that highlights the importance of a low fat diet.

Jackson (2012) …

4 A study that proves the findings of a previous study.

Tse's findings …

5 A study that shows opinions that were not known before.

The study …

Remember

✓ There are five main areas of interview questions.

✓ It is important to structure your questions clearly so that they gather the information you need and are clear for the respondent to understand.

✓ The interviewer can have an effect on how the respondent answers the questions and you may need to take this into consideration when analysing your data.

✓ Academic writing does not usually use a great range of tenses.

✓ A reporting verb + *that* is one of the most common structures for reporting in academic writing.

6 | Percentages and fractions

Aims ✓ learn how to work with percentages   ✓ compare fractions and percentages
✓ learn how to understand fractions   ✓ use verbs and nouns and dependent prepositions

Aims

Quiz
Self-evaluation

Read the statements below. Circle the answers that are true for you.

1	I understand how to work with percentages.	agree | disagree | not sure
2	I understand how to use fractions.	agree | disagree | not sure
3	I know the differences between fractions and percentages.	agree | disagree | not sure
4	I can use verbs and nouns and dependent prepositions.	agree | disagree | not sure

If you read a newspaper article, visit a website, or even walk down the high street, you will find that percentages and fractions are frequently used and written about. Here are some common ways in which we use percentages and fractions in everyday life:

to calculate discounted prices in a sale	50% off the lowest ticket price ½ price sale – now on!
to understand the instructions in a recipe	add ¾ cup of sugar
to work out the meaning of the information on food labels	contains 94.9% wholegrain wheat
to understand the results of a survey	64% of men travel to work by car a quarter of the students study English

This chapter will help you to understand what is meant when percentages and fractions are used in these types of situations. You will learn how to calculate a percentage and a fraction of a quantity and how to convert between equivalent percentages and fractions. To help when you are reading or writing about percentages and fractions, you will also practise how to use verbs and dependent prepositions.

Working with percentages

What is a percentage?

A percentage means 'part of a hundred'. The symbol % is used as a percentage sign. So if 25% of books in a library are non-fiction, it means that 25 out of every 100 books in the library are non-fiction.

You can write a percentage as a fraction : 16% is the same as $\frac{16}{100}$

You can also think of a percentage visually: in the diagram shown below, 45% of the squares are shaded, that is 45 out of 100 squares. You can see that the remaining 55 squares are not shaded, representing 55% of the total number of squares.

Exercise 1

1   In the waiting room at a doctor's surgery, 38% of the patients are male. What percentage of the patients is female?

2   In a small business, 46% of revenue is used to pay for overheads such as electricity, rental costs and wages, and the rest is profit. What percentage of the revenue is profit?

Percentages are often used to explain things in everyday life. Here are some examples of percentages that were printed in a local newspaper:

Tennis court hourly rates are set to increase by between 26 and 31 per cent, and many swimming pool charges will go up by 10 per cent.

40 per cent of pupils in the borough eat a school meal at lunchtime.

As far as land use is concerned, 50 per cent of the buildings will be used for retail outlets.

Research showed that the processing time for a report was reduced by 80%.

Students at the college achieved a 98% pass rate across 40 subject areas.

Exercise 2

Find an everyday item which uses a percentage as part of its labelling.

■   What information does the percentage tell us?

■   Can a calculation be made using the percentage?

Calculating the percentage of a quantity

You can work out the percentage of a quantity, for example 15% of £320, with or without using calculator.

allocate
If one item
or share of
something is
allocated to
a particular
person or for
a particular
purpose, it is
given to that
person or used
for that purpose.

band
A band is a range
of numbers or
values within
a system of
measurement.

Using a calculator, divide the percentage by 100 and then multiply the result by the quantity that you are interested in. So for example, 15% of £320 would be calculated as follows:

$$1 \quad 5 \quad \div \quad 1 \quad 0 \quad 0 \quad \times \quad 3 \quad 2 \quad 0 \quad =$$

Try working through this calculation using your calculator; if you have keyed in everything correctly, the result should be £48.

If you want to find the percentage of a quantity without using a calculator, the simplest method is to first find 10% of your quantity and then use this amount to complete the remaining parts of the calculation. It is easy to find 10% of a quantity because this is the same as dividing the quantity by 10. Using our example again of 15% of £320, here are the steps involved:

10% of £320 = £320 ÷ 10 = £32

5% is half of 10%, so 5% = £32 ÷ 2 = £16

15% = 10% + 5%, so 15% of £320 = £32 + £16 = £48

You can solve real-life problems using either of these methods.

Example:

A venue can seat 2,500 people. For a music concert, it is decided that the seats will be allocated to different price bands as follows:

40% for price band A

25% for price band B

20% for price band C

10% for price band D

5% for price band E

We can calculate how many seats will be allocated to each price band as follows:

10% of 2,500 = 250

5% is half of 10%, so 5% = 250 ÷ 2 = 125

price band A = 40% = 4 × 10% = 4 × 250 = 1,000 seats

price band B = 25% = (2 × 10%) + 5% = (2 × 250) + 125 = 500 + 125 = 625 seats

price band C = 20% = 2 × 10% = 2 × 250 = 500 seats

price band D = 10% = 250 seats

price band E = 5% = 125 seats

Tip ✓ When you have finished, always double check your calculations to ensure that you have not made any simple mistakes with your multiplication and addition.

Exercise 3

Use a calculator to work out:

1 36% of £500

2 45% of 620 g

3 78% of 200 m

Exercise 4

Work out these percentages without using a calculator:

1 30% of £250

2 50% of 80 kg

3 85% of 340 cm

Exercise 5

A large box of assorted chocolates contains 180 chocolates. It has:

5% orange dreams

35% fudge delights

20% nutty clusters

15% coffee swirls

25% caramel moments

How many chocolates of each type are in the box?

Percentage changes

Increases and decreases of numbers are sometimes expressed in terms of percentages. Looking back at the earlier examples from a local newspaper, we saw that:

■ Many swimming pool charges will go up by 10 per cent.

■ Research showed that the processing time for a report was reduced by 80%.

Clearly, if we know the current charge for a swim and the current processing time for a report, then it is possible to work out the new values using the percentage changes.

Example:

A bus fare of £2.60 is increased by 5%. Work out the new price of travelling on the bus.

10% of £2.60 = £2.60 ÷ 10 = 26p

5% is half of 10%, so 5% = 26p ÷ 2 = 13p

The cost increase of 5% is 13p and so the new bus fare is £2.60 + 13p = £2.73

Example:

To increase sales during the summer holiday season, the price of a car is reduced by 12%. If the original price of the car is £24,000, calculate the sale price.

10% of £24,000 = £24,000 ÷ 10 = £2,400

2% is a fifth of 10%, so 2% = £2,400 ÷ 5 = £480

so, 12% = £2,400 + £480 = £2,880

The price reduction of 12% is £2,880 and so the sale price is £24,000 − £2,880 = £21,120

Exercise 6

1 In a January sale, a shop reduces its prices by 15%. Work out the sale price of a dress which previously cost £44.

2 Tracey earns £45,000 per year. She gets a 2% pay rise. How much does Tracey earn after her pay rise?

3 The charge for a telephone call costing £4.20 is increased by 5%. What is the new charge?

Exercise 7

Complete the table below with the correct verb or noun form.

Verb	Noun
increase	
	reduction
allocate	
divide	
multiply	
	rise
calculate	

Exercise 8

Complete these sentences with the verb or noun of the word in brackets. You might need to change the tense of the verbs.

1 There was an _____ of 10% per annum. (increase)

2 Sales _____ by $500,000 dollars last year. (decrease)

3 The government _____ £2 billion for education reform programmes this year. (allocate)

4 The _____ of labour was not considered fair. (divide)

5 _____ the cost price by 1.4 to work out the mark-up required. (multiply)

6 Sales _____ by 30% in 2012. (rise)

7 Percentages are a simple _____ many people find hard to do. (calculate)

Using fractions

What is a fraction?

A fraction is a way of dividing a whole unit into equal parts. Every fraction is made up of two numbers:

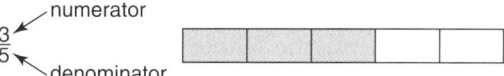

Improper and mixed fractions

For an improper fraction, the numerator is larger than the denominator. An improper fraction can be written as a mixed fraction which has a whole number and a fraction part together.

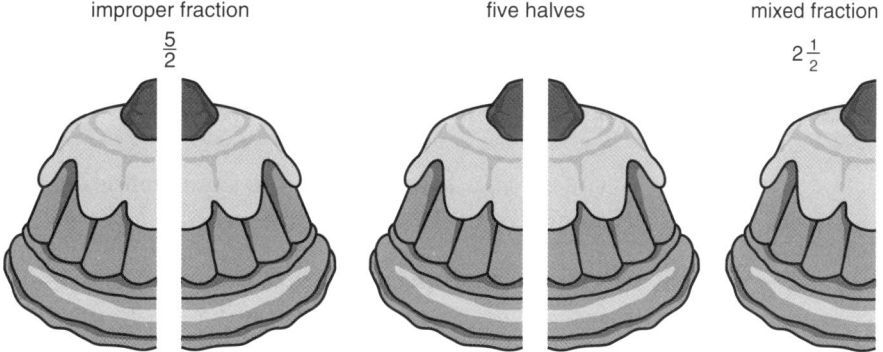

improper fraction
$\frac{5}{2}$

five halves

mixed fraction
$2\frac{1}{2}$

To convert from an improper fraction to a mixed fraction, use these steps:

1   Divide the numerator by the denominator.

2   For the first part of the mixed fraction, write down the whole number part of the answer.

3   Then write down a fraction, keeping the same denominator that you started with, but using the remainder from step 1 as the numerator.

For example, to convert the improper fraction $\frac{17}{5}$ to a mixed fraction:

1   Divide 17 by 5 to give the answer 3 (because $3 \times 5 = 15$) with a remainder of 2.

2   Write down the 3 as the first part of the mixed fraction.

3   Then write down a fraction with the same denominator of 5 and using the remainder 2 as the numerator.

So, $\frac{17}{5}$ as a mixed fraction is $3\frac{2}{5}$

To convert from a mixed fraction to an improper fraction, use these steps:

1   Multiply the whole number in the improper fraction by the denominator.

2   Add the answer from step 1 to the numerator.

3   Write down a fraction, keeping the same denominator that you started with, but using the final result as the numerator.

For example, to convert the mixed fraction $4\frac{3}{7}$ to an improper fraction:

1   Multiply 4 by 7 to give the answer 28.

2   Add 28 to 3 to give the result 31.

3   Write down a fraction with the same denominator of 7 and using the final result 31 as the numerator.

So, $4\frac{3}{7}$ as an improper fraction is $\frac{31}{7}$

Exercise 9

1   $\frac{16}{6}$ is an improper fraction. Which mixed fraction is it equal to?

a $4\frac{5}{6}$ b $8\frac{1}{6}$ c $2\frac{4}{6}$

2   $4\frac{3}{4}$ is a mixed fraction. Which improper fraction is it equal to?

a $\frac{17}{4}$ b $\frac{19}{4}$ c $\frac{14}{4}$

equivalent
If one amount or value is equivalent to another, they are the same.

Equivalent fractions

Fractions which look different but have the same value are called equivalent fractions. They represent the same part of a whole unit.

These fractions are the same because the same proportion of the shape is shaded:

$$\frac{1}{2} \qquad\qquad \frac{3}{6}$$

If you multiply or divide the numerator and denominator in a fraction by the same number, then you will find an equivalent fraction.

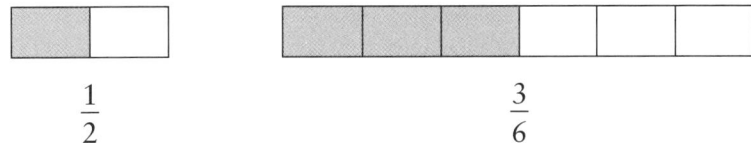

$$\frac{2}{3} = \frac{4}{6} = \frac{6}{9}$$

$$\frac{12}{36} = \frac{3}{9} = \frac{2}{6}$$

Examples:

Find the missing number for this pair of equivalent fractions.

$$\frac{5}{9} = \frac{\square}{63}$$

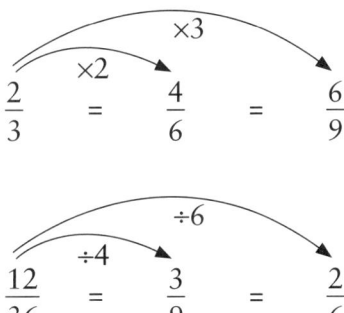

$$\frac{5}{9} \quad \text{is equivalent to} \quad \frac{35}{63}$$

Are these two fractions equivalent to each other?

$$\frac{7}{11} \text{ and } \frac{21}{33}$$

Yes, because the numerator and denominator have been multiplied by 3.

Exercise 10

Find the missing number for this pair of equivalent fractions.

$$\frac{4}{5} = \frac{\square}{30}$$

Exercise 11

Are these two fractions equivalent to each other?

$$\frac{5}{9} \text{ and } \frac{20}{36}$$

Calculating a fraction of a quantity

You can work out a fraction of a quantity by following two simple steps:

1   Divide the quantity by the denominator of the fraction.

2   Multiply the numerator of the fraction by the answer you get from step 1.

> For example, to find $\frac{3}{4}$ of 20:
>
> 1   Divide 20 by 4: $20 \div 4 = 5$
>
> 2   Multiply 3 by 5: $3 \times 5 = 15$
>
> So, $\frac{3}{4}$ of 20 is 15

Tip ✓   Always think about your answer to ensure that it makes sense. If our answer in the example above had been larger than 20, this would indicate that we had made a mistake in our calculation because a fraction of a quantity can never be larger than the quantity itself.

Exercise 12

Work out:

1 $\dfrac{2}{9}$ of 27   2 $\dfrac{3}{5}$ of 55   3 $\dfrac{4}{7}$ of 35

Comparing percentages and fractions

Percentages and fractions are two different ways of writing down the proportion of something, for example, 50% of £20 is the same as saying ½ of £20.

It is possible to convert from a percentage to a fraction and from a fraction to a percentage. The table below shows some simple conversions that you should learn:

Percentage	1%	5%	10%	20%	25%	50%	75%
Fraction	$\dfrac{1}{100}$	$\dfrac{1}{20}$	$\dfrac{1}{10}$	$\dfrac{1}{5}$	$\dfrac{1}{4}$	$\dfrac{1}{2}$	$\dfrac{3}{4}$

Tip ✓ Try to learn the conversions listed in the table above because they are very commonly used.

For other values, follow these conversion rules:

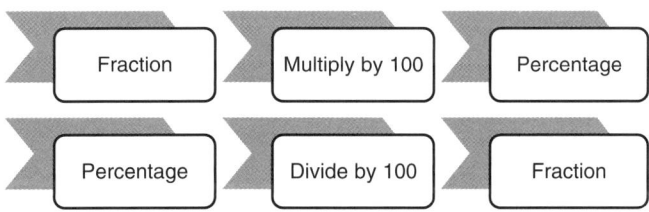

Numbers

Examples:

Convert $\dfrac{4}{5}$ to a percentage.

$\dfrac{4}{5}$ multiplied by $100 = \dfrac{400}{5} = 80\%$

Convert 65% to a fraction.

65 divided by $100 = \dfrac{65}{100} = \dfrac{13}{20}$

Exercise 13

Convert these fractions to percentages:

1 $\dfrac{6}{20}$ 　　2 $\dfrac{3}{25}$ 　　3 $\dfrac{8}{10}$ 　　4 $\dfrac{17}{50}$

Exercise 14

Convert these percentages to fractions:

1 78% 　　2 30% 　　3 85% 　　4 44%

Exercise 15

Complete the table below by converting between fractions and decimals.

Fraction	$\dfrac{1}{2}$			$\dfrac{7}{20}$			$\dfrac{11}{25}$			$\dfrac{9}{50}$	
Percentage		26%			40%			3%			65%

For more information on the grammar of fractions, see the section at the end of the book.

Exercise 16

Here are some fractions: $\frac{1}{4}$ $\frac{18}{50}$ $\frac{8}{25}$ $\frac{7}{10}$

Choose one that is:

1   equal to 32%   **2**   greater than 50%   **3**   less than 30%   **4**   equal to 36%

We can use conversions between percentages and fractions to help us to work out comparisons of numbers in everyday life. Consider the following 'special offers' advertised by two different shops:

Shop 1   Shop 2

We can convert $\frac{2}{5}$ into a percentage to compare its value to 30%. $\frac{2}{5}$ multiplied by $100 = \frac{200}{5} = 40\%$, so we now know that shop 1 is offering a better sale than shop 2.

Verbs and nouns and dependent prepositions

A number of verbs and nouns are commonly used in academic writing with particular prepositions, known as dependent prepositions. These can be used to describe the collection and analysis of data.

Exercise 17

Match these verbs with the prepositions used with them. Some verbs take more than one preposition.

~~account~~	argue	~~associate~~	attribute	~~benefit~~	compare
contrast	decrease	exclude	increase	provide	rise

for	from	to	with
account	benefit		associate

Exercise 18

Complete these sentences with collocations from Exercise 17. Sometimes you will need to change the form of the verb.

1 Older generations shop very differently _compared to_ younger generations.

2 Teenagers _____ 60% of the negative responses.

3 Twelve of the questionnaires were _____ the analysis as they were incomplete.

4 The differences in stress levels can be _____ the lower levels of exercise.

5 Previous research has _____ bonuses _____ only short-term satisfaction.

6 Satisfaction _____ its lowest level when discussing the working environment.

7 The correction rate of the first group of teachers _____ the other teachers in the study.

8 The results _____ us _____ a new understanding of the topic.

Exercise 19

Which is the correct noun form of each verb?

1	argue	a	argue	b	argument
2	associate	a	associate	b	associative
3	attribute	a	attribute	b	attributed
4	benefit	a	benefit	b	beneficial
5	exclude	a	exclude	b	exclusion
6	provide	a	provide	b	provision
7	rise	a	rise	b	raise
8	compare	a	compare	b	comparison

Exercise 20

Correct the preposition in italics in each of these sentences.

1   Respondents were asked to give an account *for* their experiences.

   Respondents were asked to give an account of *their experiences.*

2   The argument *for* the conclusion was that little evidence could be found to support the hypothesis.

3   Effort was seen as an important attribute *to* success in sport.

4   The benefits *from* increased exercise are numerous.

5   The exclusion *from* all fats in a diet is detrimental to health.

6   The provision *for* the right working conditions can increase staff productivity.

7   An increase *by* 12 per cent was seen.

8   A decrease *by* two fifths was found to have a significant impact.

Remember

✓   Work out the percentage of a quantity by dividing the percentage by 100 and then multiply the result by the quantity that you are interested in.

✓   Increases and decreases of numbers are sometimes expressed in terms of percentages.

✓   In an improper fraction, the numerator is larger than the denominator. An improper fraction can be written as a mixed fraction.

✓   To convert a fraction to a percentage, multiply it by 100. To convert a percentage to a fraction, divide it by 100.

✓   A number of verbs and nouns are commonly used in academic writing with particular dependent prepositions.

7 | Averages

Quiz
Self-evaluation

Read the statements below. Circle the answers that are true for you.

1	I understand why averages are used.	agree | disagree | not sure
2	I understand the differences between the types of average.	agree | disagree | not sure
3	I know how to use frequency tables to find averages.	agree | disagree | not sure

Glossary

mode
The mode is a value that occurs most frequently in a set of values.

median
The median value of a set of values is the middle one when they are arranged in order. For example, if a group of five students take a test and their marks are 5, 7, 7, 8, and 10, the median mark is 7.

mean
The mean is a number that is the average of a set of numbers.

In this chapter, we will consider the use of average values. When we collect data about something such as the annual income of accountants, the height of children in a class or the mathematics scores of some students, it is useful to be able to consider a numerical value that is representative of the whole group of people we are interested in. Rather than list all of the data values we have collected, we would like to be able to talk about the typical or average value. There are three types of averages that can be used: the mode, median and mean – each one is calculated and used in a different way. You will learn and practise the calculation methods in this chapter, and also explore the situations in which it is most appropriate to use the mode, median or mean.

Why use averages?

The word 'average' is often used in everyday life to describe a typical value of something.

> Examples:
>
> - *The average height of a footballer in a team is 182 cm.*
>
> - *The average daytime temperature in the UK in December is 6°C.*
>
> - *The average price of a loaf of bread in a supermarket is £1.20.*
>
> - *The average house price in Miami is $248,000.*

A collection of values or data can be described by an average which identifies a 'typical value' that is representative of the set.

When we write about averages there are two structures that we commonly use:

The average / height / of / a footballer in a team / is / 182 cm.

The average + noun + of + noun + verb + noun

or

The average / daytime temperature in the UK in December / is / 6°C.

The average / noun phrase / verb / noun

Exercise 1

Rearrange the words in the sentences below.

1   annual income in the United States / the average / is / $30,000

2   the average / 68% / of / score / the students / was

3   number of calories / consumed was / 2,200 / the average

4   the average / of / weight / the participants / was / 84 kilos

5   saving / the average / was / £30 per person

6   fall in house prices / the average / has been / $20,000

Different types of averages

The most commonly used averages are the mode, the mean and the median.

mode	the data value that occurs most frequently in the set
mean	the average of all the data in the set
median	the middle point when the data set is ordered

Each type of average requires a different type of calculation.

Mode

The mode of a set of data is the value which occurs most frequently. If no data value appears more frequently than any other value in the set, then there will be no mode.

> Example:
>
> The number of goals scored in eight football matches is recorded as follows:
>
> | 4 | 2 | 2 | 6 | 3 | 0 | 1 | 2 |
> |---|---|---|---|---|---|---|---|
>
> What is the mode for this data?
>
> Two goals were scored in each of three matches, and so the mode for this data is 2 – it is the number of goals that happens most frequently.

Mean

The mean is the most commonly used average. It is calculated using:

$$\frac{\text{sum of the data values}}{\text{number of values in the set}}$$

> Example:
>
> The number of pages in ten books chosen from a library shelf:
>
> | 352 | 425 | 124 | 635 | 225 | 412 | 362 | 345 | 198 | 357 |
> |---|---|---|---|---|---|---|---|---|---|

Calculate the mean number of pages for these books.

$$\text{mean} = \frac{352 + 425 + 124 + 635 + 225 + 412 + 362 + 345 + 198 + 357}{10}$$

$$= \frac{3435}{10} = 343.5$$

Median

The median is the middle value for a set of data that has been arranged in numerical order. For an odd number of data values, the median is actually one of the values in the set: the middle one. However, when there is an even number of values in a set, there is no actual middle value and therefore the median is calculated as the mid-point of the two values closest to the middle.

Example:

The scores in a mathematics test achieved by seven school pupils were recorded as:

| 56 | 85 | 24 | 39 | 71 | 46 | 58 |

What is the median score?

There is an odd number of data values (7), so we are simply looking for the middle score.

Arranging the scores in order gives:

| 24 | 39 | 46 | 56 | 58 | 71 | 85 |

The median is the middle score which is 56.

Example:

This data shows the maximum daytime temperature (in °C) each month for the period of one year:

| 7 | 7 | 10 | 12 | 16 | 19 | 21 | 21 | 18 | 14 | 10 | 7 |

Work out the median temperature.

Putting the data in numerical order gives:

| 7 | 7 | 7 | 10 | 10 | 12 | 14 | 16 | 18 | 19 | 21 | 21 |

There is an even number of data values (12), so we are looking for the two values closest to the middle. They are 12 and 14.

| 7 | 7 | 7 | 10 | 10 | 12 | 14 | 16 | 18 | 19 | 21 | 21 |

To find the mid-point of two values, you simply add them together and halve the result. In this example, we would use ½ (12 + 14) = 13, so the median for this data set is 13°C.

Exercise 2

Decide whether the following statements are True or False:

1   The median is always one of the data values in the set.
2   A data set might have no mode.
3   The mode and the median are always equal.
4   All of the data values are used when calculating the mean.
5   The mode is the middle value in the data set.

Exercise 3

Find the mode, median and mean for the following data set:

| 230 | 265 | 240 | 230 | 285 | 210 | 225 | 245 |

Exercise 4

Which type of average would be most suitable for each data set given below?

1   3.2   4.1   18.5   3.1   2.9   4.3   4.2
2   London, Bristol, Manchester, London, Glasgow, Birmingham
3   12   14   20   15   24   11   23

Exercise 5

Match the terms below to their definition.

1	average (noun)	a	an amount that is calculated by adding several numbers together and dividing the total by the original number of things that you added together
2	norm	b	an average standard or level
3	mean	c	the amount, level, standard, etc. that is typical of a group of people or things
4	the law of averages	d	based on calculations that show the average amount for each person affected
5	average (verb)	e	to usually do, have, involve, etc. a particular level or amount
6	average out	f	to have a particular number or amount as an average
7	per capita	g	the principle that if something with more than one possible result happens enough times, the result that you want is certain to happen at some time

When comparing the average of two different things, the following structure can be useful:

> *On average*, + data set 1 + linking word/phrase, *whereas*
> + data set 2.   *, while*
>   *, in comparison to/with*
>   *, compared to/with*
>
> ■ *On average, teenagers sleep more than eight hours per day, **whereas** adults sleep less than seven.*
>
> Note that we need a comma before the comparative phrases above.

For more information on comparative structures, see Chapter 10.

Exercise 6

Use the linking word or phrase in brackets and the prompts to compare these averages. Start with 'On average'.

1   respondents / spent / 30 minutes a day reading books, / they spent three hours a day on the internet. (whereas)

2   a graduate salary in Scotland / is / £30,000, / a non-graduate salary / is / only £25,000. (while)

3   the over-sixties / spend / £500 on internet shopping per year, / 25-35-year-olds, who / spend / £2,000. (in comparison to)

4   people / spent / £2,000 on holidays in 2011, /2012, / when people spent £3,000. (compared to)

Using frequency tables to find averages

Glossary

distribution
The distribution of something is how much of it there is in each place or at each time, or how much of it each person has.

You can still find the mode, mean and median values if your data has been presented as a frequency distribution rather than just a simple list of values.

Example:

The frequency table shows the number of goals scored in the netball games played during a local schools tournament.

Number of goals	0	1	2	3	4
Frequency	2	3	9	2	1

This table of data tells us that 17 games were played in the tournament and that:

- no goals were scored in two games

- 1 goal was scored in three games

- 2 goals were scored in nine games

- 3 goals were scored in two games

- 4 goals were scored in one game

The **mode** for this data is the number of goals that were scored with the highest frequency, that is, the number of goals per game that occurred the greatest number of times. Two goals per game were scored in nine games, so the modal number of goals is 2.

To find the **mean**, we use the same formula as before:

$$\frac{\text{sum of the data values}}{\text{number of values in the set}}$$

The numerator is calculated by multiplying each observation by the frequency with which it happens and then adding up all of these values. So in this example, it is the sum of each number of goals scored multiplied by the number of games in which it happened, as follows:

$$(0 \times 2) + (1 \times 3) + (2 \times 9) + (3 \times 2) + (4 \times 1) = 0 + 3 + 18 + 6 + 4 = 31$$

The denominator is simply the total of all the frequencies, which is the total number of games in this example:

$$2 + 3 + 9 + 2 + 1 = 17$$

So, the mean is calculated as: $31 \div 17 = 1.82$ goals

For the **median**, we need to identify the middle data value in the table. If we put our data into a list, it would look like this:

| 0 | 0 | 1 | 1 | 1 | 2 | 2 | 2 | ② | 2 | 2 | 2 | 2 | 2 | 3 | 3 | 4 |

So, the median number of goals is 2.

Exercise 7

The table below shows the number of days' absence taken by 31 pupils in a school during one term. Find the mode, mean and median number of absence days.

Number of days	0	1	2	3	4	5
Frequency	8	15	3	2	2	1

Choosing the right average to use

The mode, mean and median each have their own advantages and disadvantages.

Mode

Advantages	
The mode is easy to find.	12 9 11 9 5 6 11 8 11 7 8 No calculation is needed to work out that the mode for these ages of children is 11.
Non-numerical data can also have a mode.	cat dog hamster cat rabbit cat dog We know that the mode for these types of pets is cat even though the data is qualitative.

Disadvantages	
Not every set of data has a mode.	174 cm 163 cm 179 cm 160 cm 177 cm There is no mode in this list of heights because each value occurs only once.
The mode is not always representative of the data.	56 56 75 79 81 85 88 90 92 95 The mode of these examination scores is 56 but this score is not representative of the data.

Mean

Advantages	
The mean uses all of the values and therefore it is very representative of the data.	The calculation for the mean involves adding all of the data values together and dividing by the number of data values.

Disadvantages	
The mean is not always a data value.	5 4 6 3 1 2 1 3 3 4 2 4 1 1 The average number of children for this data set is 2.86, which is not one of the data values.
The mean can be affected by extreme values.	If we insert an extreme value of 200 in the data set above, then the mean becomes 16 because it is biased towards the extreme value.

Median

Advantages	
It is easy to find the median when data is in order.	5 6 7 8 8 9 9 11 11 11 12 No calculation is needed to work out that the median for these ages of children is 9.
The median is not affected by extreme values.	If we insert two extreme values, 200 and 300 in the data set above, the median remains unchanged as 9.

Disadvantages	
The median is not always a data value.	1 1 1 2 2 2 2 2 3 3 For the number of cars owned by each family, the median is 2.5, which is not one of the data values.
The median is not always representative of the data.	10p 12p 15p 15p 45p 78p 85p 94p 98p The median of these prices is 45p, but this price is not representative of the data.

Exercise 8

Consider which average is the best one to use for each of these three sets of data.

1   purple   red   green   orange   red   green   purple   green   green

2   25   96   22   21   20   28   29   27

3   148   141   141   146   145   143   144

Remember

✔ There are three measures of averages – mean, mode and median.

✔ Use linking phrases to compare the average of two different things.

✔ You can use frequency tables to find averages.

✔ Choose the right average for your purposes.

8 Presenting your data

Quiz
Self-evaluation

Read the statements below. Circle the answers that are true for you.

1	I understand the different ways data is presented.	agree | disagree | not sure
2	I know when and how to use each type of graphic.	agree | disagree | not sure
3	I know how to use the present simple, past simple and present perfect to describe the data presented in a graphic.	agree | disagree | not sure
4	I know how to use the active and passive voice to describe graphics.	agree | disagree | not sure

Using graphics

Glossary

visual
Visual means relating to sight, or to things that you can see.

interpreting
If you interpret something in a particular way, you decide that this is its meaning or significance.

Graphics such as graphs and charts provide a useful way of showing what your information means in a visual way. When you only have a small amount of data, a simple list may be enough for interpreting its meaning. However, if you have collected a large set of data in a survey, questionnaire or experiment then presenting it using a graphic such as a graph or chart will help you to describe your results and highlight the most important facts.

There are different types of graphics that you can choose:

- pie charts
- bar charts

- line graphs

- tables

- pictograms

- scatter diagrams

Each graphic in this list has its own advantages and disadvantages. Your choice will depend on the type of data you have collected, the audience that you are writing for, and the type of questions that you are asking about your data. The aim is to present the data in the best way for the reader to interpret.

A variety of structures and language that is used to describe graphics will be covered in the following chapters. This chapter looks at which tense to use depending on the data you are presenting. It also looks at when to use the active and passive voice.

Pie charts

Glossary

category
If people or things are divided into categories, they are divided into groups in such a way that the members of each group are similar to each other in some way.

A pie chart displays data in a circle. Each part of the circle represents the amount of data in one category. It shows each category as a percentage of the whole data set, so for example, one half of the pie chart represents 50%.

The diagram is split into sections, each one representing a different category of data. Colours, labels and an information key are used on the diagram so that the proportions can clearly be seen.

Unlike a line graph, a pie chart cannot be used to show changes that occur to data over a time period. This type of diagram becomes less useful when a data set includes many different categories of information because the circle would then be made up of too many very small sections.

Example of a pie chart

The pie chart below shows how 64 students travel to college each day.

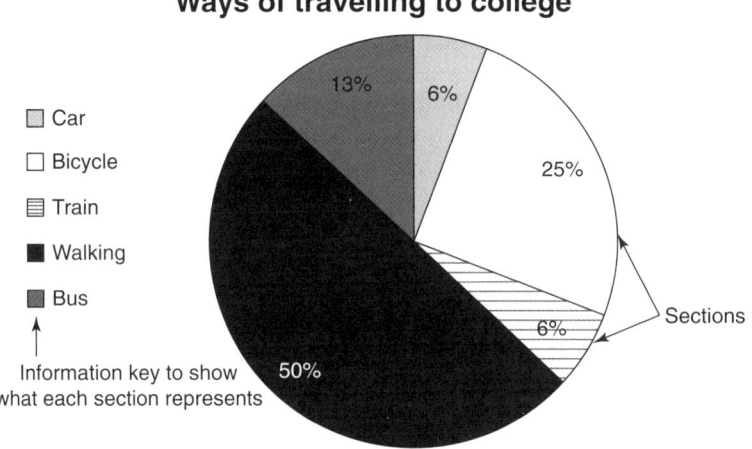

From this pie chart, we can see that:

- Walking is the most popular way of travelling to college.
- Sixteen students cycle to college each day (25% of 64 = 16).
- More students walk than use any other method of travel.
- The same number of students use a car as use the train to travel to college.
- Nineteen per cent of students questioned use public transport.
- Twice as many students walk compared to those who cycle.

Present simple

You can use the present simple to describe a number of different graphics. It very much depends on what it is that you are describing. The present simple is used to talk about things that happen all the time or repeatedly, or when something is true in general. In academic writing the most common use of the present simple is to talk about general truths. For example:

- *Macroeconomics **is** the study of the economic systems of whole countries or regions.*
- *This approach **increases** the reliability of the study.*

However, when describing graphics such as the pie chart opposite, the use can be for repeated actions:

- *Sixteen students **cycle** to college each day.*

- *Walking **is** the most popular way of travelling to college.*

Exercise 1

Complete the sentences using the present simple of the verbs in the box.

illustrate	not allow	not drive	represent	take	walk

1   The survey _____ only a small number of students.

2   The chart below _____ the most common methods of travel.

3   Half of the respondents _____ to university.

4   Only 6% _____ the train.

5   Most students _____ because the university _____ students to park on campus.

Exercise 2

Look at the pie chart and compete the description with the correct verb. More than one word may be possible.

What do you use your phone for most?

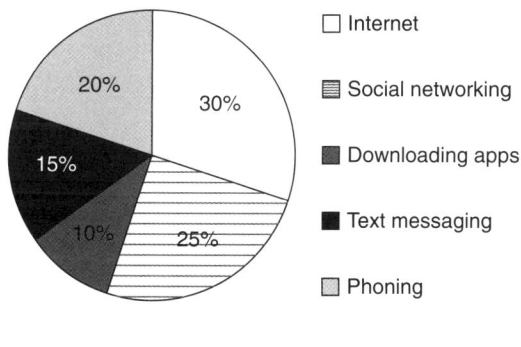

□ Internet

▤ Social networking

▦ Downloading apps

■ Text messaging

▨ Phoning

The pie chart (1) _____ the most common things people use a mobile phone for. The most common use is to (2) _____ the internet. Twenty-five per cent (3) _____ their phone mostly to (4) _____ at social network sites. The least common use is to (5) _____ apps. Only one in five people use it most frequently to (6) _____ people, closely followed by using the phone to (7) _____ texts.

Bar charts

A bar chart is a diagram drawn with rectangular bars. Each bar represents a different category in the data set. The frequency of the category is represented by the height or the length of the bar. More than one set of data can be shown on a bar chart for comparison.

The bars can be drawn vertically or horizontally. All of the bars in the chart should have equal width and be drawn equally spaced apart. The axes on the diagram should be clearly labelled, including units where necessary.

The scale on a bar chart must be carefully drawn, starting at zero, so that the diagram provides an accurate picture of the data it is representing. Be careful using 3D bar charts because the perspective of the diagram can be misleading.

Example of a bar chart

The bar chart below shows the number of visitors to a science museum from April to July last year.

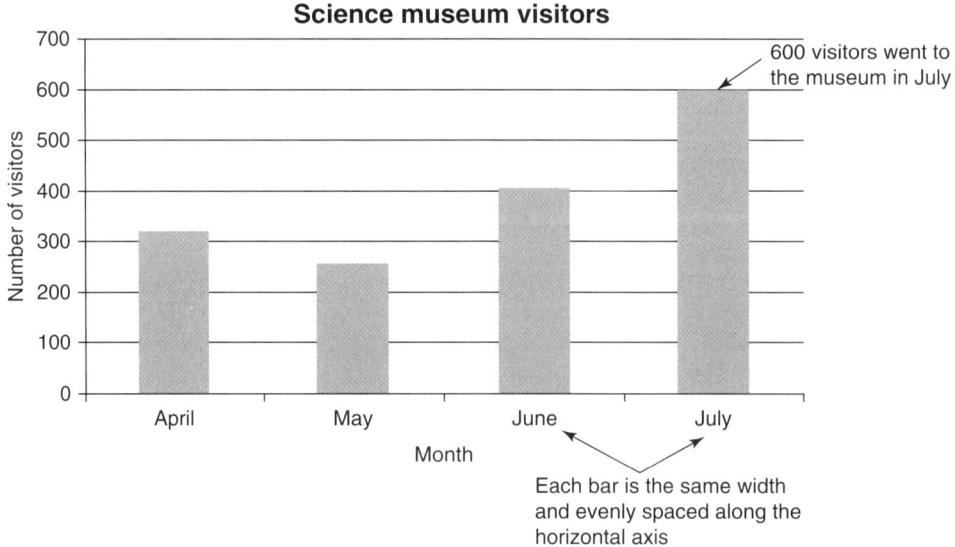

From this bar chart, we can see that:

- There were more visitors to the museum in June than in April.

- The least number of visitors went to the museum in May.

- The museum had no more than 600 visitors during any month in this period.

- Compared to July, just over half the number of visitors went to the museum in April.

- The most popular month in which to visit the museum was July.

- Over 1,500 visitors went to the museum in these four months.

The description contains a number of comparatives and superlative forms.

For more information on comparatives and superlative forms, see Chapter 10.

Past simple

This tense can be used with a number of different graphics. Use it to talk about completed actions or events, so for example, in this bar chart the data being reported is in past months and not connected to now. For example:

- *There **were** more visitors to the museum in June than in April.*

- *Over 1,500 visitors **went** to the museum in these four months.*

Many verbs end in *-ed* but there are also many other irregular verbs.

Exercise 3

Complete the sentences with the following verbs in the past simple:

be	be	double	go	increase	visit

1 There _____ just over 300 visitors to the museum in April.

2 Just under 300 people _____ the museum in May.

3 May _____ the least popular month.

4 Visitor numbers nearly _____ between April and July.

5 Numbers _____ by just over 100 between May and June.

6 Numbers _____ up in July because of the bad weather.

Numbers

Exercise 4

Complete the description of the bar chart with the verb in brackets.

Average number of customers per day

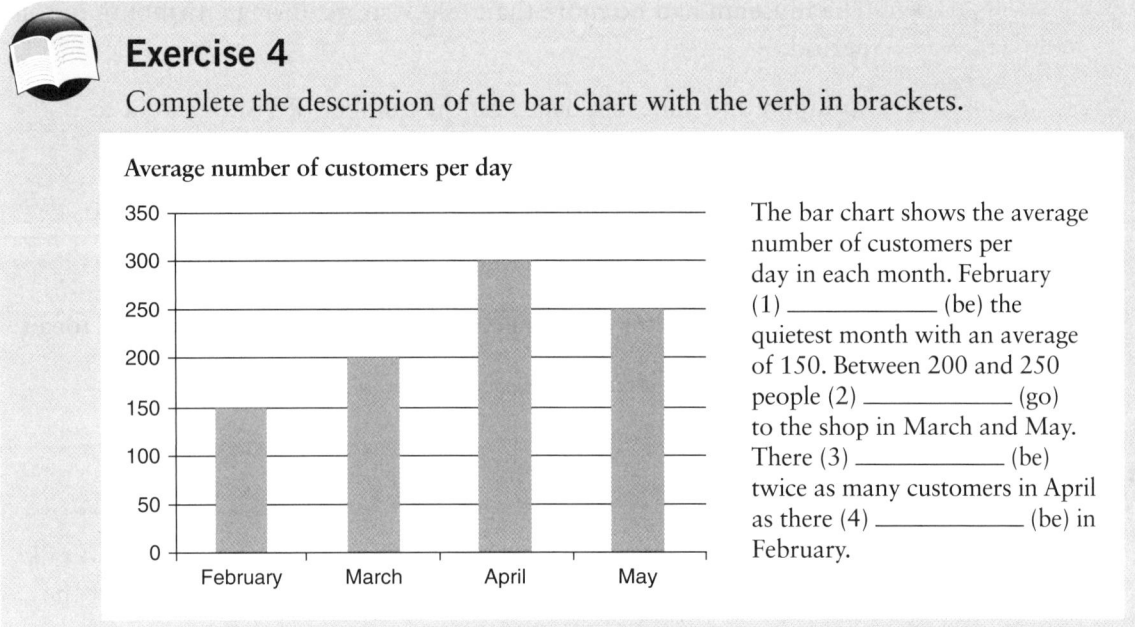

The bar chart shows the average number of customers per day in each month. February (1) _____ (be) the quietest month with an average of 150. Between 200 and 250 people (2) _____ (go) to the shop in March and May. There (3) _____ (be) twice as many customers in April as there (4) _____ (be) in February.

Line graphs

Glossary

exaggerate
If you exaggerate, you indicate that something is, for example, worse or more important than it really is.

A line graph usually has a time scale shown along the horizontal axis. This type of graph can be used to show how a set of data values changes over time. Two sets of data can easily be compared by plotting both lines on the same graph.

The points on a line graph are joined by a set of straight lines. Some examples of time periods are: minutes, hours, days, weeks, months or years. Both axes should be clearly labelled with a title and units of measurement if appropriate.

You must look very carefully at the vertical axis scale on a line graph when you are trying to interpret the trends in the data over time. If the scale is too small then the patterns in the data may be exaggerated.

Example of a line graph

The line graph below shows how the average daily temperature in the UK changed throughout one year.

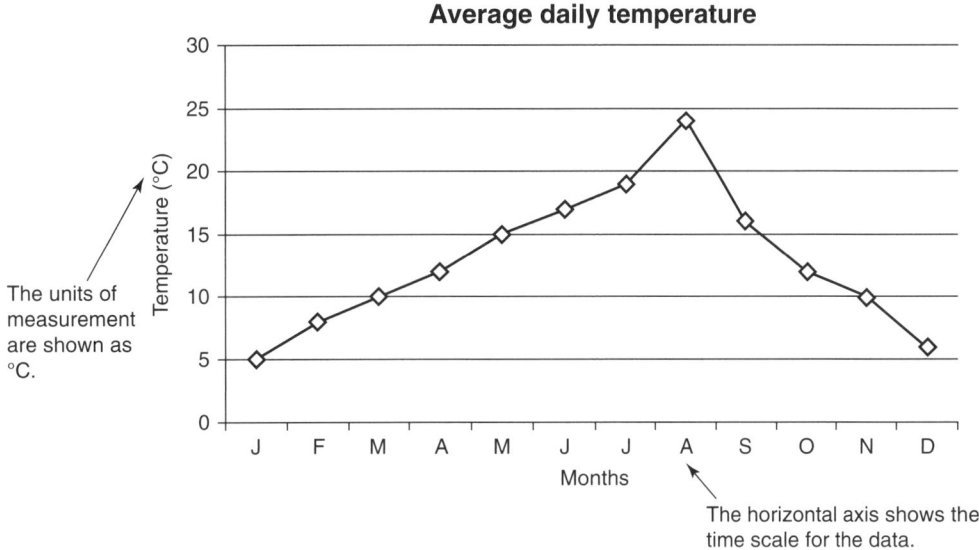

From this line graph, we can see that:

■ The average daily temperature did not fall below 5°C during the whole year.

■ Between January and August, the average daily temperature increased each month.

■ The largest fall in temperature occurred between August and September.

■ The highest average daily temperature was in August.

■ The temperatures in January were generally lower than the temperatures in December.

■ The steepest increase in temperature occurred between July and August.

Past simple versus present perfect

Use the past simple when the action or event is finished and there is no connection to now. The past simple is used to describe data from a past point in time. The present perfect is used to show data that continues up until a recent point or that is still being collected. As a result the present perfect is mainly only used when describing line graphs. For example:

- *Between January and August, the average daily temperature **went up** each month.*

Use the present perfect when there is a connection to now:

- *Temperatures **have reached** a record high.*

Compare the following:

- *Temperatures **increased** between April and June.*

- *Temperatures **have increased** since April.*

 **Exercise 5**

Complete each sentence with the present perfect or past simple of the verb in the brackets.

1   There _____ record levels of rain so far this month. (be)

2   Temperatures _____ in August last year. (peak)

3   Last month _____ as hot as May. (be)

4   To date average temperatures _____ up by 2 degrees. (go)

5   We _____ the wettest month on record. (have, just)

6   Last August the high temperatures and low rainfall _____ fires to break out in many regions. (cause)

Exercise 6

Complete the description of the line graph using the correct form of the verb in brackets.

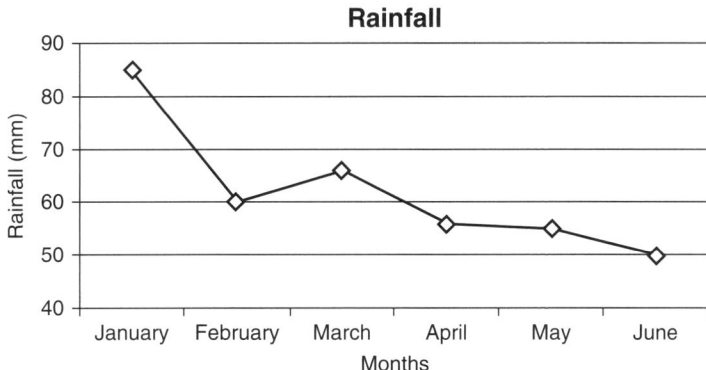

The graph shows the monthly rainfall so far this year. There (1) _____ (be) over 350 mm of rain so far this year. The heaviest month (2) _____ (be) January with 85 mm, followed by March when 66 mm of rain (3) _____ (fall). Rainfall (4) _____ (decrease) month on month for the last four months. January (5) _____ (be) the wettest month in the first six months of the year.

Tables

You can use a table to present your information more clearly. The numerical entries in the table represent the frequency of each category of data. A table is easy to create and understand.

Example of a table

The table which follows shows the data collected in a survey in which 60 schoolchildren were asked to give their favourite colour.

Favourite colour of schoolchildren

Informative title

Colour	Number of children
blue	12
pink	6
purple	11
green	8
yellow	10
red	4
other	9
Total	60

The total is 60 because this is the number of children asked in the survey

This table shows us:

- More children liked purple than pink.

- 60 children were asked about their favourite colour.

- Four children liked red.

- Twice as many children liked green compared to red.

- The most popular colour was blue.

Two-way tables

A two-way table shows the information for two linked sets of data. Once again, each entry in the table represents the frequency of a category of data.

The categories for one variable are listed as rows and the columns are used for the other variable. When you have entered all of your data into a two-way table, you should calculate the total for each row and column; the overall total must be equal to the number of data values that you collected.

Example of a two-way table

The following two-way table shows the travel destination and gender of passengers surveyed in a busy airport.

Travel destinations and gender

Each category is clearly labelled

	Female	Male	Total
USA	25	39	64
Europe	30	27	57
Australia	10	16	26
other	42	11	53
Total	107	93	200

The 'other' category represents people who were travelling to another destination

This two-way table shows us:

- 200 people were questioned in the survey.

- The most popular destination was the USA.

- 57 passengers travelled to Europe.

- 107 of the passengers questioned were female.

- More male passengers travelled to Australia than female passengers.

- 12.5% of the passengers questioned were females travelling to the USA.

Active or passive?

Both active and passive can be used with a number of different graphics. Use the active voice when you are interested in who does something:

- *More male passengers **travelled** to Australia than female passengers.*

Use the passive voice to focus on when, where or what was done rather than who did it:

- *200 people **were questioned** in the survey.*

The passive is formed with different tenses of the verb *be* + past participle:

■ *The number of laptops sold **was recorded** for three years.*

■ *Respondents are **given** 30 seconds per question.*

Exercise 7

Complete the text below with the active or passive form of the verb in brackets.

Monthly non-essential purchases and gender

	Male	Female	Total
Clothes	$100	$180	$280
Snacks and drinks	$70	$60	$130
Computer games	$150	$50	$200
Mobile phone	$30	$80	$110
Total	$350	$370	$720

Two hundred respondents (1) _____ (question) on their monthly non-essential purchases. An average of $350 (2) _____ (spend) by boys and an average of $370 (3) _____ (spend) by girls. Clothes (4) _____ (buy) most commonly by girls, whereas boys mostly (5) _____ (spend) money on computer games. The girls' mobile phones (6) _____ (cost) an average of $80 a month while the boys only (7) _____ (spend) an average of $30. A similar amount (8) _____ (spend) by both boys and girls on snacks and drinks.

Exercise 8

Put the verbs in brackets into the correct form, present simple or past simple, active or passive.

1 The scores in Social Science and English Language _____ (correlate, positively).

2 On average 70 laptops _____ (sell) every month.

3 The greatest number of passengers _____ (travel) to the USA last month.

4 Laptops _____ (be) more popular than desktop PCs.

5 No students _____ (score) less than 50% in English last term.

6 Girls _____ (achieve) higher scores in languages than boys every year.

Pictograms

A pictogram uses symbols or pictures to represent the frequency of each category in the data set. Each picture or symbol may represent one or more units of data. This type of diagram can be easier to understand and interpret.

All the symbols should be the same size on the diagram. An information key must be included so that you know the frequency that is represented by each symbol.

It can be difficult to draw part of a symbol to show every frequency value on the diagram. For example, if ☺ is used to represent 4 people, then showing a frequency that is not a multiple of 4, i.e. 11 people can be quite difficult to show accurately.

Example of a pictogram

The following pictogram shows the number of goals scored in the football matches played by a local team in their league.

Number of goals scored

This pictogram shows us:

- 21 matches were played in total by the team.

- The team scored four goals in three of their matches.

- Two goals were scored in a third of the team's matches.

- The maximum number of goals scored in a match was four.

- In five of the matches, the team did not score any goals.

- The number of goals most frequently scored was two.

Exercise 9

1   Look at the description above of the pictogram and identify whether the passive or active has been used in each sentence.

2   Why do you think the active or passive was chosen in each case?

Scatter diagrams

A scatter diagram is used to represent and compare two sets of data. Each point on a scatter diagram represents a pair of data values. By looking at a scatter diagram you may be able to see a link, or correlation, between the two variables.

If both variables increase at the same time, then they have a positive relationship. If one variable increases whilst the other one decreases, then they have a negative relationship. Sometimes there is no pattern on the diagram, showing that the variables are not correlated.

Even if a scatter diagram shows that two variables are correlated, it does not necessarily mean that a change in one variable causes a change in the other one. There is often a third variable that acts as a link but is not shown on the diagram.

Example of a scatter diagram

The scatter diagram opposite shows the percentage scores for an English Language test and a Mathematics test achieved by 20 children in the same class at school.

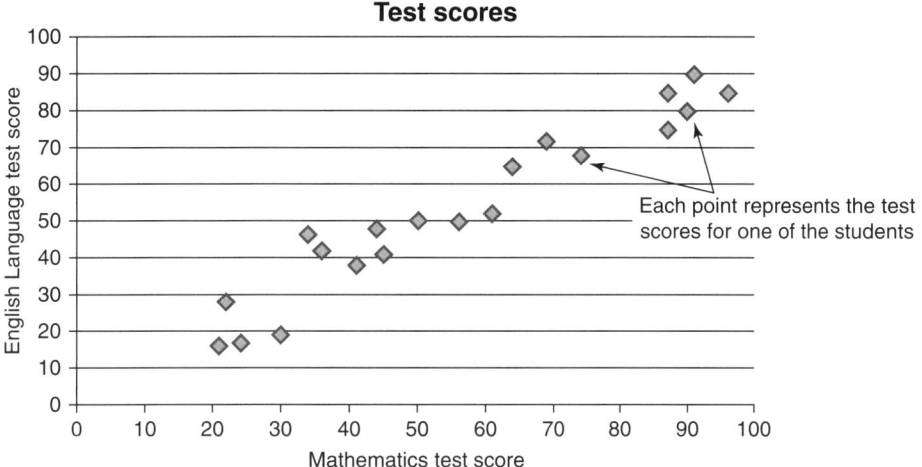

From this scatter diagram, we can see that:

- The scores in Mathematics and English Language are positively correlated.

- No student scored less than 20% in Mathematics.

- One student scored 50% in both tests.

- Students who scored highly in Mathematics also scored well in English Language.

- Three students scored more than 80% in both tests.

- Students with a low score in English Language also had a low score in Mathematics.

Exercise 10

1 Look at the description of the scatter diagram and identify the tenses used.

2 Why do you think these tenses were chosen?

Tip ✓ When choosing to present your own data, think about the best method to present it.

Tip

Exercise 11

Look at the three graphics below. The people have used the wrong type in each case. Which type should they have used?

Ages of brothers and sisters

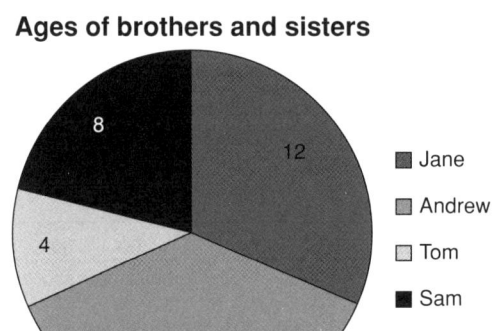

- Jane
- Andrew
- Tom
- Sam

How students spend their money

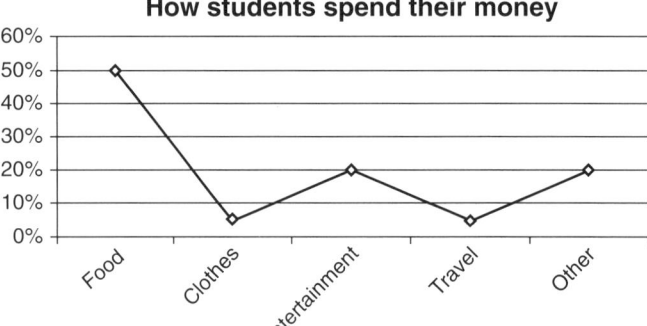

Daily hours of sunshine

	Hours of sunshine
June	
July	
August	

 Represents 8 hours

Exercise 12

Correct any mistakes in tenses in these sentences describing graphics.

1   The graphic is illustrating the most common purchases in the shop each month.

2   Sales have increased dramatically at the start of last year.

3   The website had an increasing number of hits every month this year.

4   The most common way to travel to work last month has been by car.

5   More drinks bought in May than in June.

6   Brazil was exported more coffee than any other nation last year.

7   The Chinese economy grows by 8% last year.

8   Buses have been used every day by more students than any other group.

Tip ✓ Double check your use of tenses, both passive and active, after you have written any work presenting data.

Remember

✓   Choose the correct graphic to represent your data.

✓   Choose the correct tense to describe your graphics.

✓   Use the active and passive voice correctly to describe your graphics.

9 Describing change

? Quiz
Self-evaluation

Read the statements below. Circle the answers that are true for you.

1	I know a wide range of verbs related to change.	agree | disagree | not sure
2	I can represent change visually.	agree | disagree | not sure
3	I know a wide range of adverbs to describe change.	agree | disagree | not sure
4	I can use adjective and noun combinations to describe change.	agree | disagree | not sure

Representing change visually

A time series is a set of data values that have been collected at regular intervals over a particular time period. By looking closely at the data set, we can analyse how the value of something changes over time. For example, we may be interested in the increases and decreases in the amount of rainfall in Hong Kong throughout the year.

These data values can be plotted on a **time series graph** which provides a visual representation of how the information changes over time, as shown in the following example.

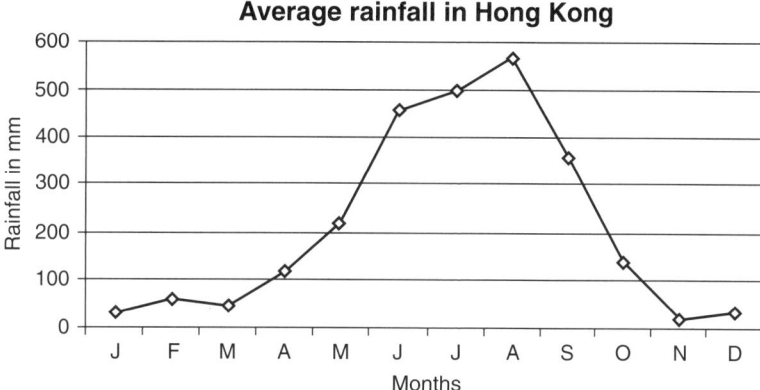

Average rainfall in Hong Kong

Time series data can be collected for a wide range of application areas. The data is usually recorded on a daily, weekly, monthly, quarterly and annual basis. Some examples are given in the following table:

Application area	Time series data
economics and finance	weekly share prices monthly sales figures annual profit or loss
meteorology	daily amount of rainfall hours of sunshine each week average temperature at night
sociology	monthly crime figures unemployment rates each quarter population growth over a decade
travel	weekly number of rail passengers annual airline fuel consumption number of road traffic accidents each year
education	number of university applicants each year weekly class attendance records quarterly expenditure figures for schools

Numbers

Data collected throughout a specific time period can be analysed so that we can make predictions about future information. This is known as forecasting, and may allow us to make decisions about events in the future. For example, if a business can predict its fuel costs over the next three years, then the management may be able to calculate the value of sales needed to generate a profit. Various types of patterns or features can sometimes be seen when the data values are plotted on a time series graph. Investigating these patterns may help us to make sense of the data and explain why there are fluctuations at certain points in the time period. We will focus on trend and seasonal variation.

Trend can be described as the general direction in which the data values are heading over the time period that the data was collected. The direction might be increasing, decreasing or remaining constant. Although there may be temporary variations at certain points on the graph, trend is the basic drift of the data set. A trend line can be applied to a time series graph; it is like a line of best fit through the data points and can be drawn 'by eye', making sure that there are an equal number of data points above and below the line.

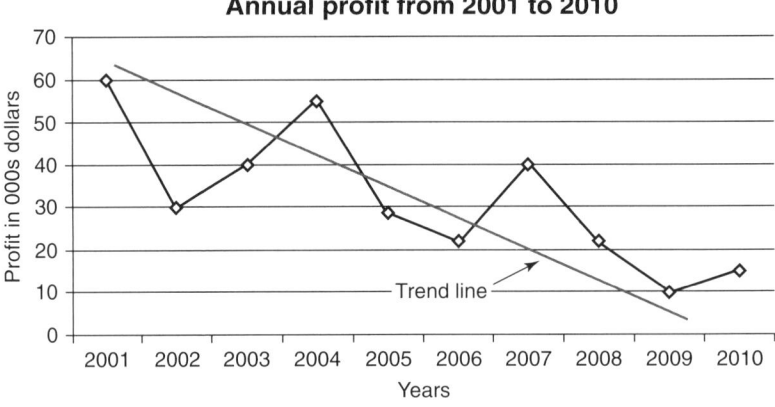

The diagram above shows the annual profit for a manufacturing firm over a period of ten years. A trend line has been applied to make it easier to see the overall direction of change in profit over the whole time period. The trend line can be used to make a general prediction about future profit for the organization. In this case, although there are increases and decreases in profit during the ten years, the general trend suggests that profits will continue to decrease overall.

The values of time series data can have a regular pattern where increasing and decreasing fluctuations appear in cycles. These patterns are known as seasonal or cyclical variation and usually continue throughout the entire time period in which the data was collected, and most likely, beyond. Seasonal variations are often related to changes in temperature, so for example, the average household heating costs in the UK will be higher in autumn and winter than in spring and summer, with the highest costs occurring between December and February and the lowest costs in June to August; this pattern will repeat itself every year regardless of the actual monetary cost. This example is illustrated in the time series graph below.

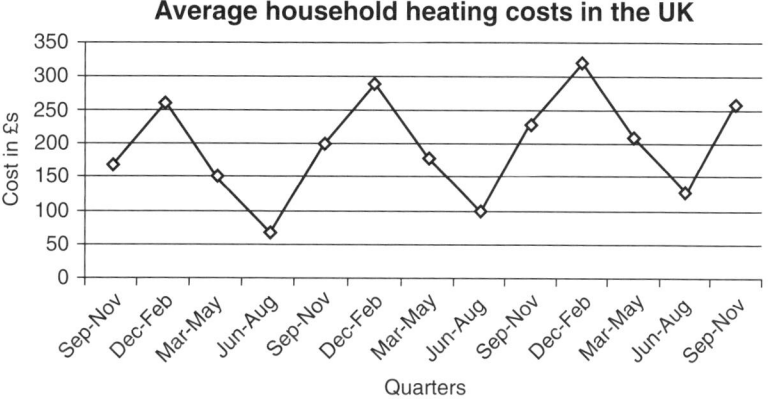

When you create a time series graph, sometimes you will be able to identify an overall trend and some seasonal variation for your plotted points. Look again at the diagram above which shows average household heating costs in the UK. You should be able to see that, in addition to the seasonal variation we have identified, there is also an overall trend towards increased heating costs over the time period in which the data was collected.

In summary, this section has illustrated how a time series graph can help us to:

- describe the general trend of the data values

- identify any cyclical patterns that exist in the data

- make decisions about the future based on the historical data.

Exercise 1

Using the time series graph shown below, describe the seasonal variation in the number of unemployed school leavers.

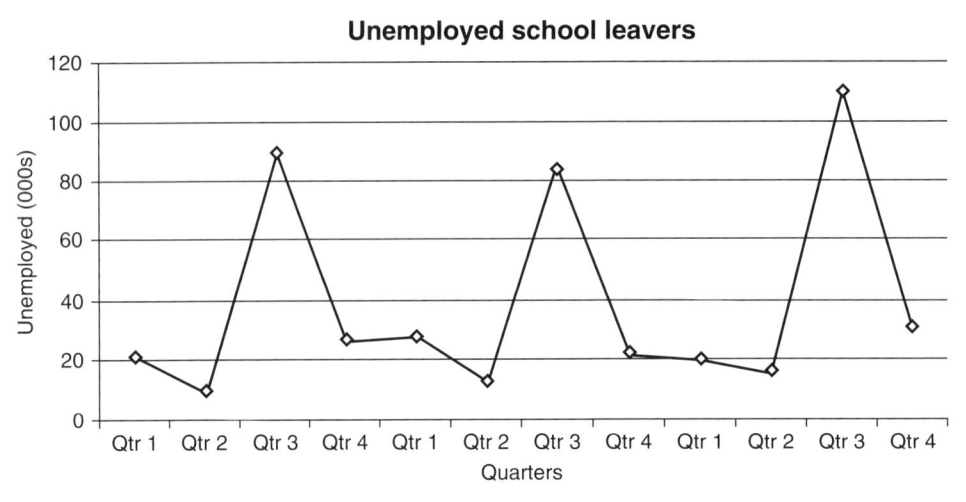

Exercise 2

Using the time series graph shown below, describe the overall trend in the number of visitors to a popular theme park in Spain.

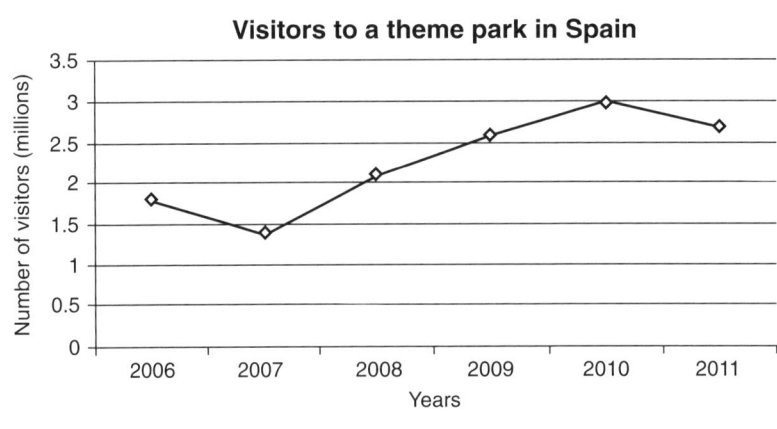

Verbs of change

A wide range of verbs can be used to describe change. Some of these verbs will perhaps be more commonly used to describe a graph or a trend that represents your data set, but verbs of change can be used to describe many aspects of the research process. For example:

■ *After piloting the questionnaire, three of the questions were **altered**.*

■ *The research question was **revised** after completing the literature review.*

Exercise 3

Match the verbs in the box to the functions. More than one verb is possible for each function.

decrease	diminish	distort	include	incorporate	increase	modify	rise

1 make different

2 less

3 more

4 bring together

There are a number of verbs in addition to those above that can be used to describe when something is more or less. For example:

Verbs for upward trends

increase, rise, go up, peak, improve, gain, recover, soar, skyrocket

Verbs for downward trends

fall, drop, plunge, plummet, decline, decrease, dwindle, slump

For same / unchanged trend

level off, stabilize

Words such as *soared, skyrocketed, plunged* and *plummeted* are quite informal. When we want to describe the rate or the significance of a change we tend to add an adverb to a simple verb like *increase*. See the next section for further work on this.

Exercise 4

Complete these sentences with verbs from the list in Exercise 3. More than one verb may be possible and you might need to change the tense.

1   Sociologists predict that the number of people taking drugs to help raise exam performance _____ from 7% to 15% next year.

2   The poor sampling is likely to have _____ the results.

3   The effect _____ and became less significant as more was added.

4   In general the interview pilot was successful, but one or two questions were _____ for clarity.

5   Age was not _____ as a factor.

6   The results from the three stages are _____ in the chart below.

7   It was observed that heart rates _____ significantly further after 30 seconds of activity.

8   The results showed that a reduction in sleep _____ the participants' ability to concentrate on the tasks and results were consequently down.

Adverbs to describe change

Verbs of change can be further described by adding a relevant adverb to the verb. For example:

- *Stress levels **varied** only **slightly** between members of the control group. However, these levels **fell dramatically** in the unhealthy group after a period of exercise.*

Exercise 5

Look at the adverbs in the box below. Which ones indicate a large difference and which ones indicate a small difference?

considerably	dramatically	marginally	noticeably	sharply
significantly	slightly	somewhat	steadily	to a small degree

Large difference	Small difference
considerably	*slightly*

Exercise 6

Look at the four graphs which follow and answer the questions on the next page.

1

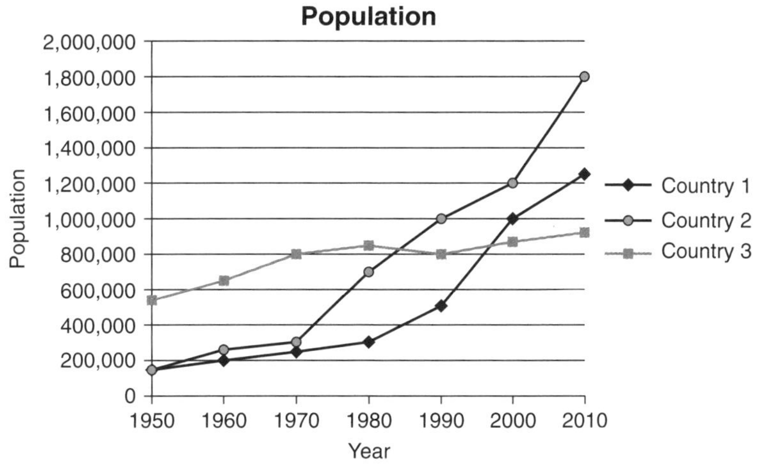
Population
2,000,000
1,800,000
1,600,000
1,400,000
1,200,000
1,000,000
800,000
600,000
400,000
200,000
0
Population
1950
1960
1970
1980
1990
2000
2010
Year
Country 1
Country 2
Country 3

2

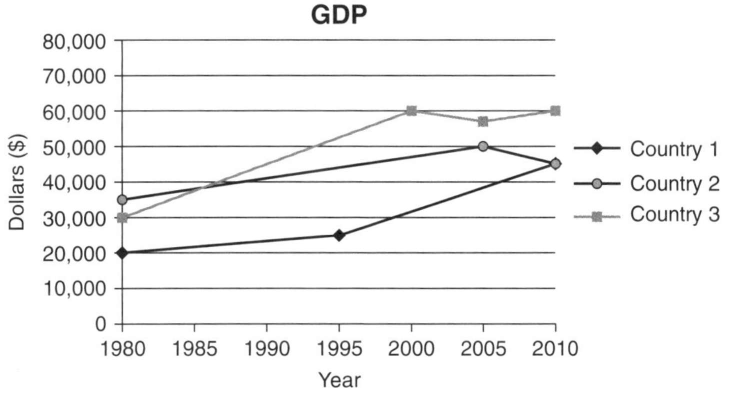
GDP
80,000
70,000
60,000
50,000
40,000
30,000
20,000
10,000
0
Dollars ($)
1980
1985
1990
1995
2000
2005
2010
Year
Country 1
Country 2
Country 3

3

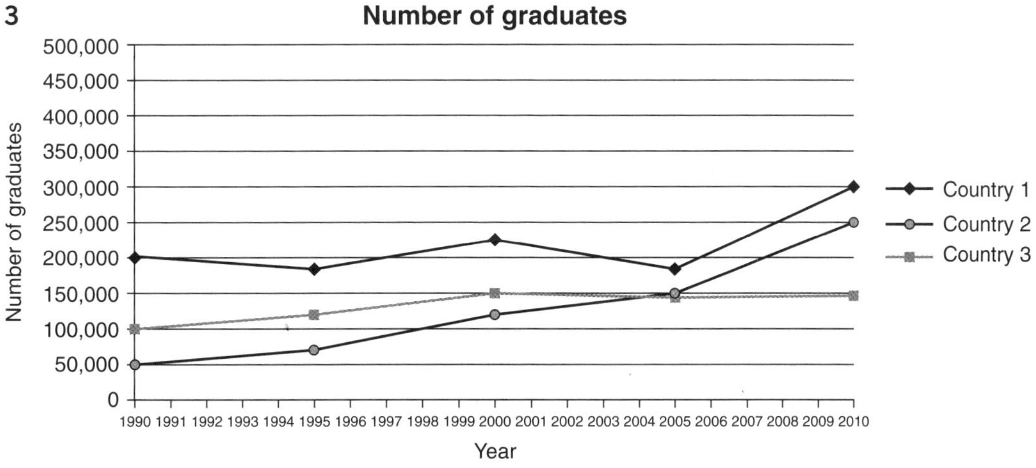
Number of graduates
500,000
450,000
400,000
350,000
300,000
250,000
200,000
150,000
100,000
50,000
0
Number of graduates
1990 1991 1992 1993 1994 1995 1996 1997 1998 1999 2000 2001 2002 2003 2004 2005 2006 2007 2008 2009 2010
Year
Country 1
Country 2
Country 3

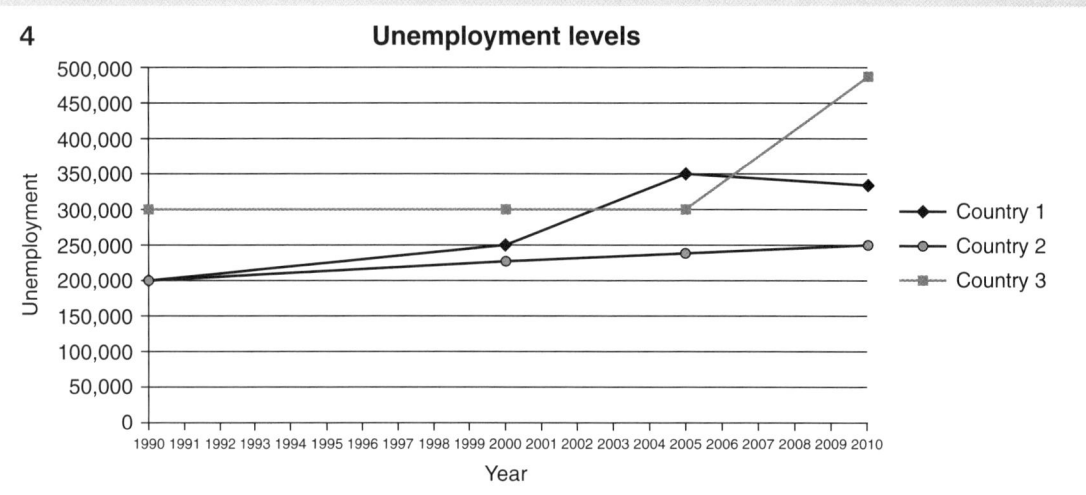

4   **Unemployment levels**

Legend: Country 1, Country 2, Country 3

1 In which country does the population level increase dramatically between 1990 and 2000?

2 In which country does the GDP fall slightly between 2000 and 2005?

3 In which country does the number of graduates not increase significantly between 2005 and 2010?

4 In which country does the population increase considerably between 1960 and 1980?

5 In which country does GDP increase considerably between 1995 and 2010?

6 In which country does the number of graduates fall marginally between 2000 and 2010?

7 In which country does the number of graduates increase steadily between 1990 and 2010?

8 In which country does the level of unemployment increase noticeably between 2000 and 2005?

9 In which country does unemployment increase sharply in the final five years?

10 In which country are unemployment levels somewhat stable?

Exercise 7

Complete these sentences about the graphs in Exercise 6.

1 The population of Country 2 _____ between 2000 and 2010.

2 The population of Country 1 _____ between 1950 and 1970.

3 The GDP of Country 2 _____ between 2005 and 2010.

4 The GDP of Country 3 _____ between 1980 and 1995.

5 The number of graduates in Country 1 _____ between 1990 and 1995.

6 The unemployment levels in Country 2 _____ between 1990 and 2010.

Exercise 8

Look at the graph below and use the adverbs in the box to write your own description of each factor. More than one adverb may be possible.

marginally	noticeably	sharply	somewhat	steadily

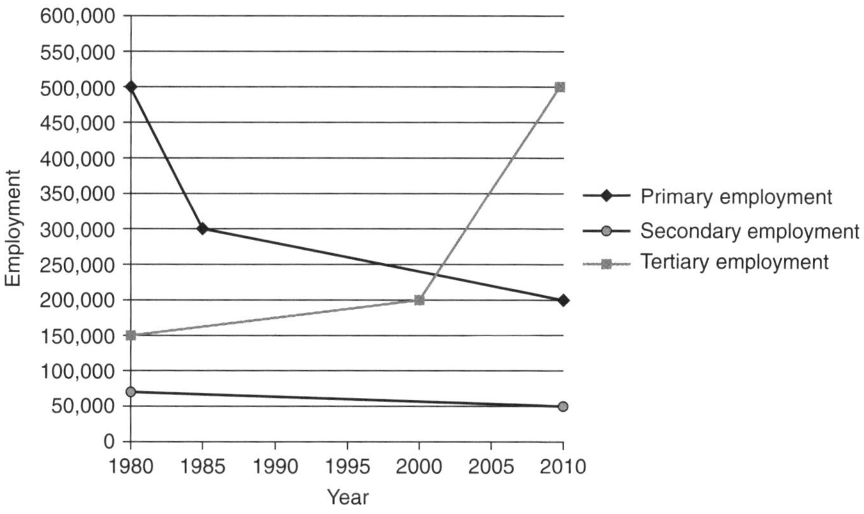

A line graph with Employment on the y-axis (0 to 600,000) and Year on the x-axis (1980 to 2010), showing Primary employment, Secondary employment, and Tertiary employment.

1   The change in secondary employment between 1980 and 2010.

2   The change in primary employment between 1980 and 1985.

3   The change in tertiary employment between 1980 and 2000.

4   The change in primary employment between 1985 and 2010.

5   The change in tertiary employment between 2000 and 2010.

Adjective and noun combinations

Many nouns also describe change. Sometimes the noun form is the same as the verb form, for example: decrease, increase, fall. However, with other words the verb and noun form change, for example: improve – improvement, expand – expansion. These nouns can be combined with adjectives to describe the change further.

Numbers

Exercise 9

Complete the table below with the noun form of each verb.

Verb	Noun
modify	
decrease	
increase	
distort	
incorporate	
rise	
include	
decline	
grow	
improve	
expand	

Exercise 10

Complete these sentences with the correct form of the word in brackets.

1 There was a _____ fall in the level of unemployment. (steady)

2 The significance of each factor _____ as the experiment continued. (diminish)

3 The _____ of the sample size made the data more representative. (expand)

4 There has been a _____ improvement in the standard of living. (marginal)

5 The _____ of higher levels of salt in diets was a key factor. (include)

6 The _____ of the two questions meant that clarity was less of an issue. (modify)

7 There has been a _____ fall in the pass rate. (sharp)

8 The closure of the mining industry _____ increased unemployment in this sector. (dramatic)

Exercise 11

Match the adjectives below to the definitions.

1	gradual	a	happening quickly and unexpectedly
2	sudden	b	a change or difference that is very obvious and easily noticed
3	marked	c	a change or process that occurs in small stages over a long period of time
4	steady	d	something that happens all the time or is always there
5	constant	e	a change which continues or develops gradually without any interruptions

Remember

✓ Use time series graphs as an effective way to represent change visually.

✓ Use verbs and adverbs of change correctly to describe change.

✓ Use nouns and adjectives correctly to describe change.

10 | Making comparisons

✓ use graphics to compare information

✓ use comparative structures

✓ use superlative structures and cautious language

Quiz
Self-evaluation

Read the statements below. Circle the answers that are true for you.

1	I understand how to use graphics to compare information.	agree | disagree | not sure
2	I know how to use comparative structures.	agree | disagree | not sure
3	I know how to use superlative structures and cautious language.	agree | disagree | not sure

Using graphics to compare information

Glossary

shading
If you use shading on a chart, you colour an area darker than the surrounding areas, so that it can be distinguished from them.

Chapter 8 introduced a variety of different types of graphics that can be used for displaying information in a visual way. This chapter will help you to evaluate which of these graphics are appropriate for comparing several sets of data at the same time.

We are often interested in analysing information about two sets of data to be able to make comparisons and draw conclusions. For example, we may be interested in contrasting the performance of boys and girls in a school mathematics test, or we might wish to observe the variation in the amount of daily sunshine between New York, London and Sydney.

A bar chart with two or more bars for each category of data can be used to compare multiple sets of data on the same diagram. This type of bar chart is known as a **multiple bar chart**. It is helpful to use shading or colouring to distinguish between the different data sets and a key is essential for explanation.

Consider the data shown in the table below.

	Average test score in mathematics	
	Boys	Girls
Green Hill School	72%	56%
West Park School	87%	67%
New Town School	58%	62%

The following multiple bar chart can be produced using this data:

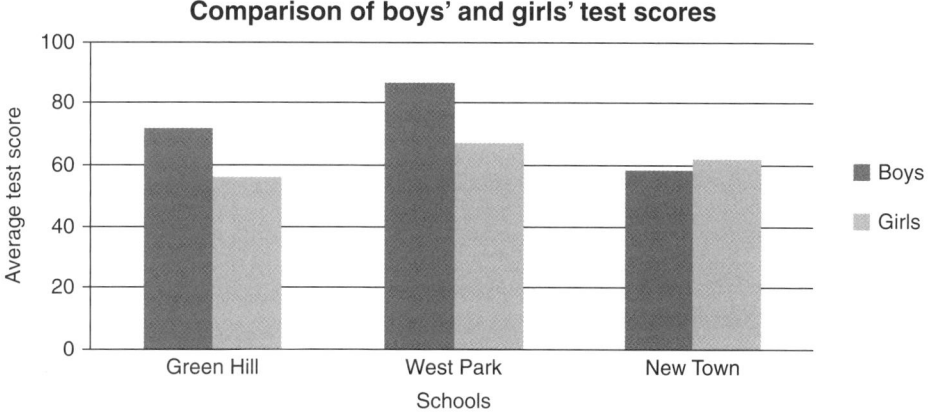

Just by visually comparing the heights of the paired bars for each gender, we can immediately observe that the average score for boys was higher than for girls at both Green Hill School and West Park School. It is also clear that whilst girls achieved a higher average score than boys at New Town School, the difference between the genders was smallest at this school.

If you have collected several sets of data that occur at regular intervals over a specified time period, then a time series graph can be used to illustrate and compare this information. Returning to the example about variation in the amount of sunshine, look at the data shown in the table on the next page.

	Average daily sunshine hours		
	New York	London	Sydney
January	6	9	9
February	6	9	8
March	7	10	8
April	8	11	8
May	9	12	7
June	11	14	7
July	11	14	7
August	10	13	9
September	9	12	9
October	7	10	9
November	6	9	9
December	5	9	9

The time series graph below shows this data visually.

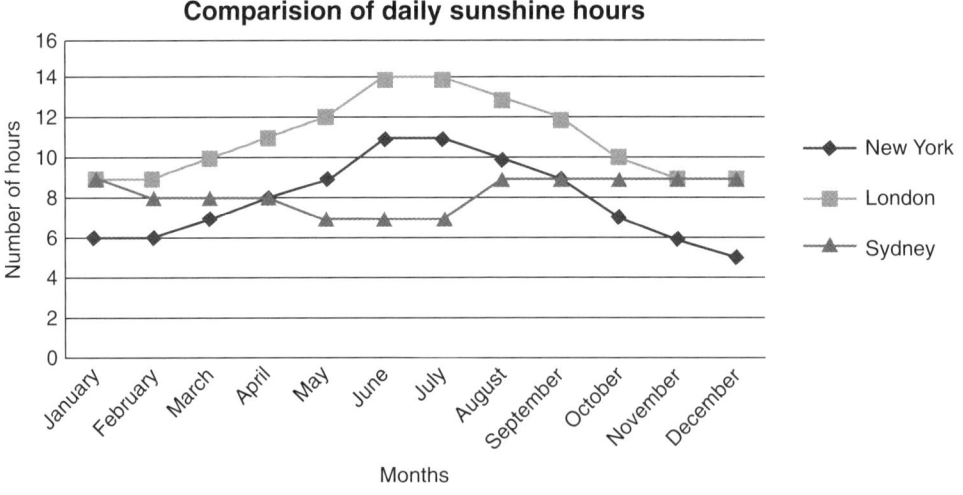

By displaying the information from all three data sets on a single diagram, we are easily able to highlight the differences between the amounts of daily sunshine across the three locations. It is clear from the graph that:

- Throughout the period May to August, London has the highest average and Sydney has the least daily sunshine hours.

- In April and September, Sydney and New York have exactly the same average daily sunshine hours.

- The average amount of sunshine in New York was lower than the values for London throughout the whole year in which data was collected.

Exercise 1

Decide if a time series graph or a multiple bar chart would be the most appropriate graph for the following collections of data:

1   Annual sales figures for three branches of a large furniture store for the past ten years. Each branch is located in a different county in the UK.

2   The average retirement age for men and women at five different types of supermarkets.

3   The number of hours of television watched on each weekday by adults and by children.

4   The height in centimetres of four different varieties of daffodils when measurements were taken each day for two weeks.

Using comparative structures

When you have collected data, you will often need to write about and discuss different factors that you want to compare. These differences can sometimes be some of the most interesting findings. You can use a variety of structures and language to make comparisons, as follows.

Comparative adjectives and adverbs

The comparative form of an adjective is:

adjective + -er + than

or:

more + adjective + than

One-syllable words add *-er*:

high > higher   old > older   fast > faster

You also add *-er* to two-syllable words when they end in *-y*:

easy > easier   early > earlier

Use *more* or *less* for other words with two or more syllables:

more comfortable   more expensive   less interesting

With adverbs that end in *-ly* we also use *more* or *less*:

more cautiously   more carefully   less quickly

Some words have the same form for both comparative adjective and adverb:

e.g. *fast, slow, high, low, early, late*

- *She can jump **higher** than her brother.* (comparative adverb)

- *This shelf is **higher** than the others.* (comparative adjective)

With some two-syllable words it is possible to use *-er* or *more/less*:

quieter / more quiet

Some adjectives and adverbs are irregular in the comparative form:

good/well > better   bad/badly > worse

Exercise 2

Complete these sentences using a comparative form of the words in the box.

accomplished	deep	good	happy
high	long	motivate	technological

1 Bonuses brought only short-term satisfaction whereas the positive effects of praise lasted _____.

2 Psychologists understand depression _____ than they understand happiness.

3 Social networks are likely to make people _____ than wealth.

4 Many people are _____ by the pursuit of money than friendship.

5 Being _____ in the field we specialize in is likely to lead to greater levels of satisfaction.

6 Bhutan ranks low in terms of wealth but much _____ in terms of happiness.

7 Exposure to _____ lifestyles can lead to changes in our attitude to traditional values.

8 Motivated by the amount of interesting finds just below ground level, archaeologists decided to dig _____ into the soil.

Exercise 3

Read the situations and complete the sentences that follow, using the comparative form of the adjective or adverb in brackets.

1 Children often get up at 6 a.m. Teenagers often get up at 10 a.m. (late)

Teenagers often *get up later than children.*

2 Some teenagers need 12 hours' sleep. Some adults need 8 hours' sleep. (long)

Some teenagers need to _____

3 Group A travelled an average of 5 kilometres. Group B travelled an average of 6.4 kilometres. (far)

Group B _____

4 Group A lowered their cholesterol by 10%. Group B lowered their cholesterol by 7.5%. (far)

Group A _____

5 The average score in the test was 54%. The average score in coursework was 69%. (low)

Students _____

6 IT consultants ranked first in stress levels. Teachers ranked second in stress levels. (stressed)

IT consultants _____

You can also use a number of adverbs before the comparative adjective or adverb to change the emphasis in the meaning. For example:

- *The results were **slightly** different compared to the control group.*
- *There were **much** more varied responses to question 2.*
- *Students wrote **much** better essays after they had taken the class in writing techniques.*

Other examples include *a lot, far, a bit, a little, significantly, considerably.*

You can use *the … the* when one variable is dependent on another. For example:

- ***The older** the respondent, **the more varied** the response.*
- ***The higher** the temperature **rose, the slower** the movement became.*
- ***The more** the participants slept, **the less** coffee they drank at work.*

This structure is particularly useful when discussing a correlation or a cause and effect relationship in the research.

For more information on adverbs to describe change, see Chapter 9.

For more information on correlation, see Chapter 11.

For more information on the language of cause and effect, see Chapter 12.

Exercise 4

Use the words in brackets to complete the sentences in a logical way.

1   Teenage responses to facial expression are _____ than adult responses. (much, emotional)

2   Teenagers pursuing a wider range of leisure activities are _____ to develop their brains more. (far, likely)

3   Google uses a _____ logo to appeal to people's design sense. (slightly, modified)

4   A _____ price will often make a brand's value worse. (considerably, low)

5   Reactions to the second campaign were _____. (significantly, good)

6   Responses were _____ in the second group. (a little, slow)

Exercise 5

Use the words in brackets to complete the sentences.

1   The more time children spend on hobbies, sports and homework, _____ they are. (happy)

2   The more time children spend playing video games, watching TV and socializing, _____ they are. (negative)

3   The older you are, _____ you process reactions. (carefully)

4   The more choice people have, _____ it is to make decisions. (difficult)

5   The more tired you are, _____ it is to concentrate in exams. (hard)

6   The more successful a small business is, _____ the chance it will be taken over. (great)

Prepositional structures

The prepositions *between, of, to* and *with* are commonly used with other words to make comparisons.

When there are two different things being compared, we can use the structure *comparison between … and …*. For example:

■   *This article will look at a **comparison between** the US **and** UK school systems.*

When we want to compare different examples of the same thing we can use the structure *comparison of*. For example:

■   *This article will look at a **comparison of** some of the most popular teaching methodologies.*

Both prepositions *to* and *with* can be used following *compare*. Arguably there is little difference between the two, but a slight distinction can be made in meaning.

To is often preferred when the similarity between two things is the point of the comparison. *With*, on the other hand, suggests that the differences between two things are as important as, or more important than, the similarities. However, the majority of the time there is little or no difference in meaning.

When different groups of people or things are compared we can use *similarities/differences between*. For example:

- ***Similarities and differences between** people with intrinsic and extrinsic motivation in the language classroom will be compared.*

When we compare different aspects of one thing we can use *similarities between / differences in*. For example:

- *This study will look at the **differences in** managerial styles and the output of work.*

Linking expressions

A wide range of linking expressions can also be used to show similarities and differences between things or people. Conjunctive adverbs are often used to link two independent clauses, but they can appear at the beginning, middle and end of a clause. These include:

in addition, therefore, furthermore, moreover, besides, also, too, on the other hand, in contrast, however, nevertheless, instead, still

They are separated by a comma when they appear at the beginning of a clause. For example:

- ***However**, not all participants agreed.*

They are also separated by two commas in the middle of a clause when their meaning appears to be separate:

- *Their decision, **however**, was final.*

Note that *too* cannot go at the beginning of a clause.

These words can also connect two independent clauses, preceded by a semi-colon:

- *There was a vast range of opinions; **furthermore**, there was little consistency between any two sets of opinions.*

Co-ordinators, including *and, or, but, so, for, yet* and *both*, can be used to connect words or phrases and independent clauses. When connecting two independent clauses, place a comma before the connector:

- *The deforestation of the Himalayas has led to flooding, **and** inadequate flood defences have made the problem worse.*

And can be followed by *also* as well:

- *Old age impacts on physical abilities **and also** on the mental capabilities of older people.*

Subordinators are words used to link a dependent clause to an independent clause. The dependent clause would not make sense on its own. Subordinators include:

although, though, even though, whereas, while, if, unless

- ***Although** prices rose over the six-month period, sales increased.*

We put a comma after a dependent clause but not in front of it:

- *Sales increased over the six-month period **although** prices rose.*

Note that *while* and *whereas* are used at the beginning of a dependent clause to introduce information that contrasts with the main clause:

- *The first two services are free, **while/whereas** the third costs £35.*

- ***While** the numbers of such developments are relatively small, the potential market is large.*

For more information on expressing links and connections, see Chapter 11.

Glossary

whereas
You use whereas to introduce a comment which contrasts with what is said in the main clause.

while
You use while at the beginning of a clause to introduce information which contrasts with information in the main clause.

Exercise 6

Complete the sentences with phrases from the box.

a comparison of	different from	differences in	distinguish between	similarities between

1 The data shows that there are _____ the groups.

2 _____ teaching methods and their effectiveness in vocabulary learning will be carried out.

3 The results showed a number of _____ student results.

4 Some people find it hard to _____ individual sounds.

5 The two sets of results were _____ each other.

Exercise 7

Read the paragraph below, paying attention to the words in bold. Put the words in bold into the correct column in the table below.

Both design and ease of use influence our impression of new technology. **However,** usability has often been given more importance than design. In certain situations this is understandable; **instead** of a beautifully designed door, people generally prefer one that is easy to open. **In contrast,** many people would prefer beautifully designed clothes **in comparison to** having functional clothes. In certain cases, research has shown that **as well as** having a product that functions well, design is **also** important. For example, a less attractive computer might function better **compared with** a more beautifully designed one, but people react more positively to the more beautiful design. **Likewise,** the same can be said about many cars. Owners of certain cars such as the Mini and the Beetle are in part enthusiasts of these cars because of the iconic design. **While** some people might be won over by design, others care more about performance. However, if a company can match up both, such as Apple with its iPad, then it no longer becomes a question of design **rather than** performance.

Similarities	Differences
both	*however*

Exercise 8

Link the pairs of sentences together using the word in brackets.

1   Clear skin, a small nose and chin, well-defined cheeks and large eyes are seen as attractive features in a woman. Male faces seen as attractive contain many of these features. (also)

   Clear skin, a small nose and chin, well-defined cheeks and large eyes are seen as attractive features in a woman. Male faces seen as attractive also contain many of these features.

2   Some people might feel that the obsession with attractiveness is a relatively new phenomenon. It is actually a biological factor determining survival and success.

   _____ (however)

3   The face conveys information about age and health. It conveys information about fertility.

   _____ (also)

4   Good skin condition is a reliable indicator of a strong immune system. A symmetrical face is perceived as a sign of good health.

   _____ (likewise)

5   People often think of certain physical features as key to attractiveness. Research now indicates that unique features might make people more attractive.

   _____ (whereas)

Exercise 9

Complete these sentences with the correct word.

1   Many participants failed to _____ between the options available.

    a   differ   b   differentiate   c   contrast

2   Many people cannot _____ between healthy and unhealthy options.

    a   differ   b   compare   c   distinguish

3   The _____ between the two groups is noticeable.

    a   contrast   b   comparison   c   compare

4   There is an important _____ between healthy and unhealthy fats.

    a   distinguish   b   differ   c   distinction

5   Companies must not _____ between people by age when employing someone.

    a   distinguish   b   discriminate   c   compare

6   There are many _____ between some of the common theories of motivation.

    a   similarities   b   same   c   common

7   Britain's economy used to be based on manufacturing, _____ today it is mainly a service industry.

    a   compared   b   whereas   c   whereby

Using superlative structures and cautious language

Glossary

superlative
The superlative form of an adjective or adverb is the form that indicates that something has more of a quality than anything else in a group. For example, 'biggest' is the superlative form of 'big'.

The superlative form is: *adjective/adverb* + *-est*

or: *most* + *adjective/adverb*

We use *-est* with short words of one syllable:

quick > quickest   long > longest   hard > hardest

With two-syllable words ending in *-y* we add *-est* and change *-y* to *-i*:

luck > luckiest   early > earliest

With words of two or more syllables we use *most*:

most significant   most important   most interesting

In academic writing, we do not need to express ourselves cautiously when we are talking about facts, for example, recorded data:

- *The **longest** time recorded was 2 minutes 43 seconds.*

Glossary

stance
Your stance on a particular matter is your attitude to it.

modesty
If you write with modesty, you use impersonal and cautious language in your writing.

hedging
Hedging language is language which you use to avoid answering a question or committing yourself to a particular opinion or decision.

However, when we give our opinion we often use a stance adverb with the superlative adjective to add caution to our opinion:

■ *Perhaps the most significant outcome is the importance of feedback.*

This is done because data can often be interpreted in different ways and different conclusions reached. Therefore, we are indicating that we do not necessarily consider this to be 100% the most significant factor. By making allowances for other possible interpretations and outcomes in our writing in this way we are expressing modesty, which is important if we want to speak with authority when giving our opinion.

Structures such as *stance adverb + superlative adjective* are often called cautious language or hedging language. Other structures to add caution to our writing are:

Hedging verbs
■ *The programme **appears to** have been a success.*

Modal verbs
■ *It was felt that this **might** result in a reduction of criminal activity.*

Qualifying expressions
■ *To **a certain extent** the project has achieved its aims.*

Adverbs and adjectives
■ *Apparently, a number of participants rarely attended sessions.*
■ *One **possible** solution might be to provide payment for attending training.*

Exercise 10
Complete these sentences using a superlative form of the words in the box.

careful	easy	expensive	significant

1　The _____ item most people had purchased was a house.

2　People are _____ when purchasing new technology.

3　Making purchases under $20 was considered the _____ decision to make.

4　The _____ factor when choosing a new car was the energy efficiency.

Exercise 11

Use the adverb and the superlative form of the adjective in brackets to complete the sentences.

1 _____ characteristic of a good manager is empathy. (arguably, important)

2 _____ issue was in maintaining control of the group. (potentially, problematic)

3 _____ issue was how to manage conservation. (perhaps, interesting)

4 Twenty species are _____ with extinction. (possibly, threatened)

5 The president's stance on health was _____ her _____ campaign issue during the elections. (probably, popular)

Exercise 12

Complete the following hedging words and phrases.

1 w _ _ _ d   6 in a s _ _ _ _

2 o _ _ _ _ t to   7 in s _ _ _ re _ _ _ _ _ s

3 s _ _ _ing _ _   8 it is c _ _ _ _ _ d

4 r _ _ _ ly   9 it is c _ _ _ _ _ _ _ ed

5 b _ _ _ ly sp _ _ _ _ _ g   10 it could be a _ _ _ _ d that

Remember

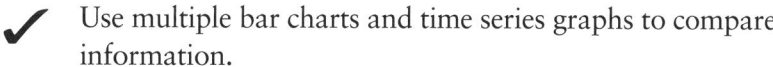

✓ Use multiple bar charts and time series graphs to compare information.

✓ Use comparative structures to discuss links between data in your research.

✓ Remember to use cautious language when you give your opinion in order not to make your statements too strong.

11 | Making connections

Aims ✓ understand correlation   ✓ express links and connections
      ✓ understand the effect of sample size ✓ describe facts and data

Aims

? Quiz
Self-evaluation

Read the statements below. Circle the answers that are true for you.

1	I understand how to identify correlations.	agree	disagree	not sure
2	I understand the effects of sample size.	agree	disagree	not sure
3	I know how to make connections between data and evidence.	agree	disagree	not sure
4	I can describe facts and data using a variety of structures.	agree	disagree	not sure

The focus of this chapter is to explore some of the important connections that can be identified when we are handling data. The first section is all about making an assessment of the type of relationship that can be identified between two different variables. This relationship is known as correlation and can be observed visually from a graph of the data. We then move on to discuss the size of the sample that is chosen from a population when you are carrying out an investigation. It is important here to establish a balance between the cost of sampling and the usefulness of the sample data for making judgements about the whole population. In the final sections of the chapter, we explain the ways in which you can use language to express the connections that you have found during your investigation so that you will be able to fully describe your ideas.

Correlation

In Chapter 8, we described how a scatter diagram could be used to represent and compare two sets of data. Each point on a scatter diagram represents a pair of data values.

By plotting one variable on the x-axis and the second variable on the y-axis, the relationship between the two variables may be seen in the pattern formed by the points on the diagram. This connection between the two variables is known as correlation.

The correlation between two variables can be described as positive, negative or no correlation.

If two variables are positively correlated this means that the value of one variable increases as the value of the other variable also increases. A typical scatter diagram showing this relationship would look like this:

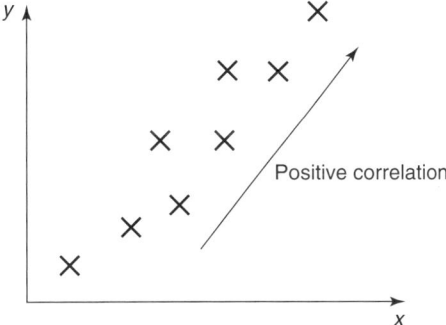

In this diagram, you can see that the points lie roughly on a straight line, indicating a linear relationship between the variables. The upward slope of the straight line shows the positive correlation between the variables.

A typical scatter diagram for variables that are negatively correlated is shown below. Negative correlation means that the value of one variable increases as the other one decreases.

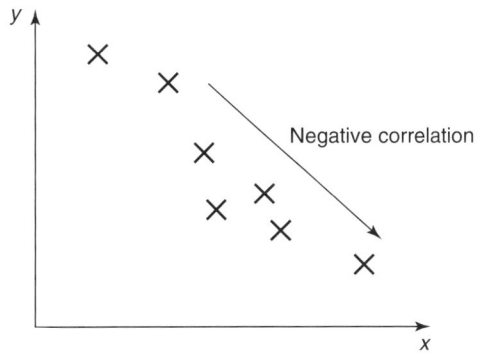

Once again, there is evidence of a linear relationship because the points on the diagram lie roughly on a straight line. Negative correlation is indicated by the downward slope of the straight line.

Sometimes the points are too scattered about on the diagram to show a linear relationship. In this situation, there is no straight line pattern and we can conclude that the variables are not correlated. A typical scatter diagram showing the data points for two variables with no correlation is as follows:

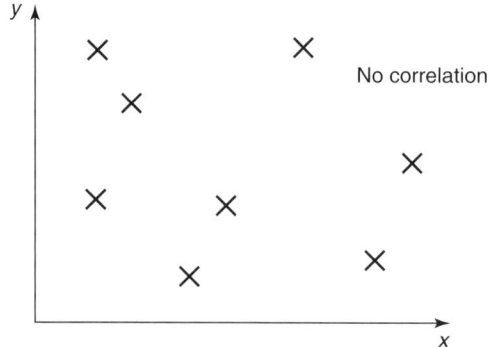

It is possible to make an assessment about the type of correlation between two variables by simply considering what you would expect to happen to the value of one variable as the value of the other variable increases. Consider the following three pairs of variables:

age of schoolchildren	positive correlation	Generally, we would expect that as schoolchildren get older, they would also grow taller.
height of schoolchildren		

daytime temperature	negative correlation	Generally, we would expect that as the temperature in the day becomes warmer, fewer scarves are sold.
number of scarves sold		

length of arm	no correlation	There is likely to be no relationship between the number of books owned by a person and the length of their arm.
number of books owned		

There is one major limitation of correlation that we should keep in mind when we are describing the type of relationship between two variables. Even if a scatter diagram shows that two variables are correlated, it does not necessarily mean that a change in one variable causes a change in the other one. There is often a third variable that acts as a link but is not shown on the diagram.

Consider this example. The scatter diagram below shows the data observations of two variables recorded during one week in December. The variable plotted on the x-axis is the number of tins of soup sold in a supermarket and the variable on the y-axis is the average household heating bill.

The pattern of the plotted points indicates that the two variables are positively correlated. However, we cannot conclude that an increase in one variable causes an increase in the other. Both of the value increases are probably caused by a decrease in daytime temperatures during that week in December.

Exercise 1

State whether you think the following pairs of variables are likely to be:

- positively correlated

- negatively correlated

- not correlated

1 depth of ocean water and amount of light measured

2 size of population in a town and crime rate

3 price of a jacket and the number of jackets sold

4 number of brothers and grade in a mathematics test

5 age and percentage of people who wear glasses

Numbers

Exercise 2

Look at these two scatter diagrams and complete the statements given below.

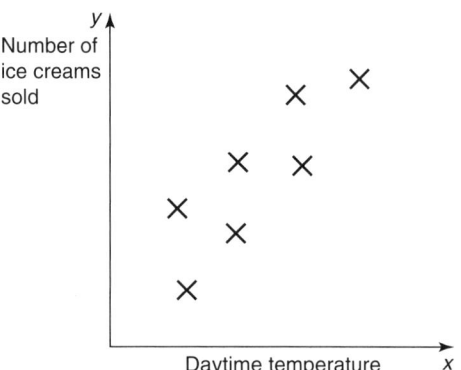

The average daily temperature and the number of ice creams sold are (1) _____ correlated. This means that as the average daily temperature (2) _____ , the number of ice creams sold (3) _____ .

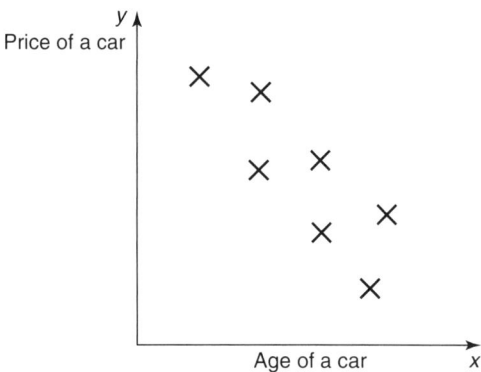

The age of a car and its price are (4) _____ correlated. We can see from the scatter diagram that the price of a car (5) _____ as its age (6) _____ .

For more information on language to discuss correlation, see Chapter 10.

Understanding the effect of sample size

When you wish to conduct a survey, it is not always possible or practical to ask everyone in your population to complete the set of questions you have devised. It is more likely that you will select only a certain proportion, or sample, of people from your population to take part in the survey.

We have already discussed some of the different ways in which you can choose your sample in Chapter 4, where we noted the importance of ensuring that the sample is a good representation of the population so that any observations made about the sample can be generalized to the population.

Determining an appropriate sample size is also a significant issue to consider. Sample sizes that are too large will mean that the survey is time-consuming and expensive to conduct, whereas choosing a sample that is too small may mean that any resulting observations are inaccurate because the sample was not sufficiently representative of the entire population. For example, if we wish to investigate the spending habits of all the residents of a large town, we would generally produce a more accurate estimate of the population values by choosing a sample size of 2,000 people rather than 20 people.

There is no simple rule for working out the best sample size for a particular investigation. For small populations, it might be possible to use the entire population as the sample, that is, by conducting a census. Using this method you will be able to make the most accurate observations because data is collected about all of the individuals. In practice, for larger populations, it is likely that the number of people selected will largely be determined by the resources – time and money – available for conducting the survey.

Expressing links and connections

A wide range of verbs can be used with prepositions to express links and connections in your research. These verb-preposition collocations can be used to connect data, evidence, people and things.

For more information on linking expressions, see Chapter 10.

Exercise 3

Match the prepositional phrases to their definition.

1	reveal links between	a	join together
2	piece together	b	show some connections
3	correlate with	c	gradually discover
4	bring together	d	talk about or mention a particular topic
5	refer to	e	connect with or relate to someone or something
6	associate with	f	show close similarity or connection with something

A number of other words and expressions can also be used to show connections between different things. Look at the next exercise and practise using the vocabulary to make connections.

Exercise 4

Complete these sentences using collocations from Exercise 3.

1 Each experiment allowed for the bigger picture to finally be *pieced together*.

2 Most management courses _____ studies in motivation, such as Maslow and Herzberg.

3 Citizen science data _____ migration and disease in monarch butterflies.

4 The characteristics people _____ one country form the basis of most stereotypes.

5 This paper aims to _____ data from various studies on metabolic rate and sugar consumption.

6 The scientist could not _____ the new data _____ his hypothesis.

Exercise 5

In each pair of sentences match the definition (a or b) to the sentence it relates to.

1   Paris has always been *synonymous with* elegance, luxury and style.

2   The exhibition in Cologne was *accompanied by* a volume of essays.

   a   Happens or exists at the same time.

   b   The two things are very closely associated with each other so that one suggests the other or one cannot exist without the other.

3   Ganley said he'd seen no *evidence of* widespread fraud.

4   A unit is *equivalent to* a glass of wine or a single measure of spirits.

   a   Anything that you see, experience, read or are told that causes you to believe that something is true or has really happened.

   b   One amount or value that is the same as another.

5   The *interaction* between mother and baby is key to emotional development.

6   The body and the mind *interrelate*.

   a   The process by which different things affect each other or change each other.

   b   A connection between two or more things that have an effect on each other.

7   There will be a written examination to *complement* the practical test.

8   A *combination of* factors caused the collapse of the economy.

   a   A mixture of things.

   b   Things that are different or do something different, which makes them a good combination.

Describing facts and data

We can talk about facts, data and evidence throughout the research process. A wide range of expressions can be used to describe how we acquire the data, the quality of the data and what the data means. The following section will give you a range of language to talk about your data and evidence. For example:

Gathering the data

■   *Data was **obtained** from national records.*

145

Quality of the data

- *The experiment was replicated four times to make the data more* **reliable**.

Interpreting the data

- *The results* **suggest** *that more infrequent vocabulary lowers motivation.*

Exercise 6

Put the words below into the appropriate column in the table.

| accurate | analyse | ~~comprehensive~~ | demonstrates | empirical | indicates |
| interpret | ~~organize~~ | record | ~~reflects~~ | shows | |

Quality of the data	Gathering the data	Interpreting the data
comprehensive	*organize*	*reflects*

Exercise 7

Read the sentences below. Which ones express a positive interpretation of the evidence, and which ones express a negative interpretation?

1   There is *growing evidence* that younger generations will live shorter lives than their parents.

2   There is *widespread evidence* that childhood obesity leads to weight issues in adult life.

3   There is *powerful evidence* that voter apathy stems from a lack of credible politicians.

4   The *evidence* for a link between hard work and success is *flimsy*.

5   Many health studies, such as the positive and negative effects of red wine, produce *conflicting evidence*.

6   There is *abundant evidence* that a sedentary lifestyle is one of the main contributory factors in many health issues today.

7   A *lack of hard evidence* was the foundation of many people's misgivings.

Remember

✓ Use a scatter diagram to show positive, negative or no correlation between variables.

✓ Keep in mind that correlation between variables does not necessarily mean that a change in one variable causes a change in the other one.

✓ Sample size can have a significant impact on the usefulness of your data.

✓ Use verb-preposition collocations to express links and connections between data, evidence, people and things.

✓ Use appropriate expressions to talk about the gathering, interpretation and quality of your data.

12 | Working with collected data

Aims ✓ learn how to present survey results   ✓ express generalizations and specifics
      ✓ avoid producing misleading results   ✓ use language of argumentation
        from diagrams   ✓ use evaluative language
      ✓ describe cause and effect   ✓ learn how to write conclusions

Quiz
Self-evaluation

Read the statements below. Circle the answers that are true for you.

1	I understand how to interpret survey results.	agree | disagree | not sure
2	I understand how to interpret results and identify if they are misleading.	agree | disagree | not sure
3	I can describe cause and effect relationships using a variety of language.	agree | disagree | not sure
4	I can talk about generalizations and specifics.	agree | disagree | not sure
5	I can use a range of language to present my arguments.	agree | disagree | not sure
6	I can use a range of evaluative language.	agree | disagree | not sure
7	I know how to structure and write a conclusion.	agree | disagree | not sure

Glossary

ambiguous
If you describe something as ambiguous, you mean that it is unclear or confusing because it can be understood in more than one way.

The aim of this final chapter is to bring together all of the different elements that you have learnt in previous sections so that you can use language, visual methods and numerical techniques to evaluate the results of an investigation and communicate your conclusions to a wider audience. Conducting a piece of research in an area of interest can be a fascinating and satisfying activity, and one of the most important aspects of the research is the analysis of the data collected and the way in which you present the evidence to support your arguments.

Throughout an investigation, you will invest substantial time in designing and carrying out the data collection and in using some of the techniques described in Chapters 6–11 to analyse your information. It is therefore essential that you choose the graphics and summary statistics that are appropriate for your type of data, and that you use the correct language so that your results are not misleading or ambiguous. This chapter will provide you with the tools required towards the end of your investigation and will help you to avoid some of the common mistakes that are made when drawing conclusions.

Presenting survey results

Once you have completed your survey and collected all the relevant information from your participants or through observations, it is then time to interpret the results. The aim of this stage in the investigation is to make sense of the facts, opinions and measurements you have gathered. Effective analysis of the sample data will allow you to extend your findings to reach generalized conclusions about the population from which the sample was selected. You will probably want to summarize what you have discovered by writing a report, displaying details on a website or giving a verbal presentation to an interested audience. Whichever method you choose to reveal your results, there are two main ways in which you can present them to help other people to understand your meaning – graphical representation and summary statistics.

Graphical representation

In Chapter 8 we investigated how graphics can be used very effectively to give a visual representation of information, particularly if you have conducted a large-scale survey.

For qualitative data where the information cannot be expressed in numerical values, the most appropriate diagrams for displaying the frequency of the results are pie charts and bar charts. As an example, consider the graphics overleaf which contain the results of observing the different coloured cars parked in a supermarket car park.

Car colour	Number of cars
red	74
black	126
silver	62
blue	41
other	29

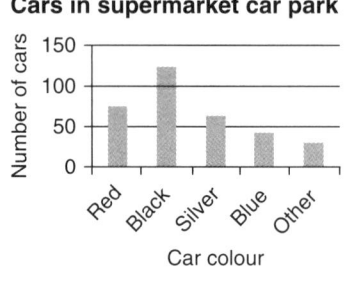

Cars in supermarket car park

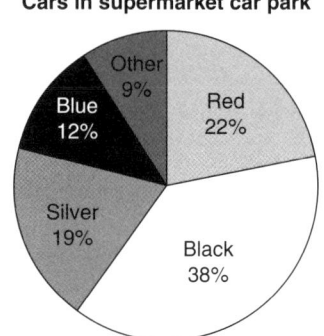

Cars in supermarket car park

The pie chart shows the proportions of each coloured car whilst the bar chart allows us to compare the actual numbers counted.

If you have collected quantitative data which can be expressed using numerical values, you will be able to choose from a wider variety of graphics to display your information. Consider using a time series graph if your data has been collected at regular intervals over a time period, or a scatter diagram if the information consists of a pair of data values such as height and weight. For simple data like the number of goals scored or the number of daylight hours, a bar chart may be the most straightforward diagram, and a pie chart should be used whenever you are investigating proportions of a whole.

Whichever graphic you choose for displaying your results, make sure that it is appropriate for the type of data, accurately drawn with sensible scales, and clearly labelled.

Summary statistics

In addition to graphics, you can use summary statistics to highlight features in the information you have collected. The following table provides some examples of numerical measures that can be used to summarize data. You can see that the median and mean averages cannot be used with qualitative data – the median requires data to be numerically ordered, and the mean calculation involves addition and division of numerical values.

Numerical measure	Examples	
	Quantitative	Qualitative
count	16 out of 25 children have at least one pet.	29 out of 100 shoppers have brown hair.
percentage	14% of the trees are less than 3 metres tall.	89% of workers travel to the office by car.
mode	Most families living in Forest Avenue have two cars.	Jane is the most common name given to baby girls.
median	The middle weight of the competing athletes is 76 kg.	✗
mean	On average, there are 17 strawberries in a box.	✗

For more information on how to calculate percentages, see Chapter 6.

For more information on how to calculate mode, median and mean average values, see Chapter 7.

Remember that the results you produce and the conclusions drawn from any investigation will only be accurate and useful if the original survey was conducted sensibly. Factors to consider include:

■ making sure your sample is representative of the entire population

■ using an adequate sample size so that statistical results are meaningful

■ designing survey questions so that they are unambiguous and not biased

When you are describing your results, you should always include some information about the factors listed above. For example, with a questionnaire-based survey you should explain how you chose your sample participants, how many people completed the questionnaire, and which questions (if any) caused confusion. Providing these details will help to put your results in context and lead to a clearer understanding of the conclusions to the investigation.

Misleading results

We have seen in previous chapters that graphs and charts which are drawn carefully and accurately can be very powerful tools for displaying and comparing information. However, sometimes diagrams can be misleading, resulting in an incorrect interpretation of the original data.

There are three main areas to consider when trying to avoid the production of a misleading graph or chart:

- visual perspective

- missing information

- the scale on the vertical axis

You may choose to draw your bar chart or pie chart as a three-dimensional diagram to make it look more attractive. This approach can make it difficult for the data values to be accurately read from the diagram, and can also make some of the bars or pie chart sections look bigger than they actually are, in proportion to the others.

The bar charts below have been drawn with exactly the same data about the number of ice creams sold.

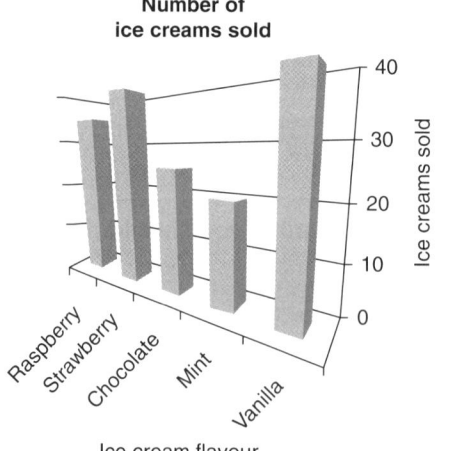

There are two main problems with the diagram on the left.

It is difficult to accurately read the data values associated with each flavour of ice cream because the bars are not lined up horizontally with the figures on the scale; it looks as though the number of vanilla flavoured

Glossary

rotate
When something rotates or when you rotate it, it turns with a circular movement.

distort
If something you can see or hear is distorted or distorts, its appearance or sound is changed so that it seems unclear.

misread
If you misread something that has been written or printed, you look at it and think that it says something that it does not say.

ice creams sold is more than 40, but in fact, using the diagram on the right you can see that the sales figure is exactly 40.

Also, the rotated three-dimensional perspective distorts the way in which we compare relative heights of the bars in the chart; it looks as though more vanilla ice creams were sold compared to strawberry ones, but the bar chart on the right clearly shows that the same number of these flavours was sold.

When creating any type of graphic it is very important that you include all the details that are needed for someone else to read the information on the diagram accurately and effectively. These details should include informative labels on both axes or all sections of the diagram, all available data, a key to distinguish between categories or data sets, and a meaningful title. If any of this information is missing, then the data values on your diagram could be misread or misinterpreted and incorrect conclusions could be drawn about an investigation.

Consider the following examples in which some information has been omitted.

Number of visitors to Kings Castle

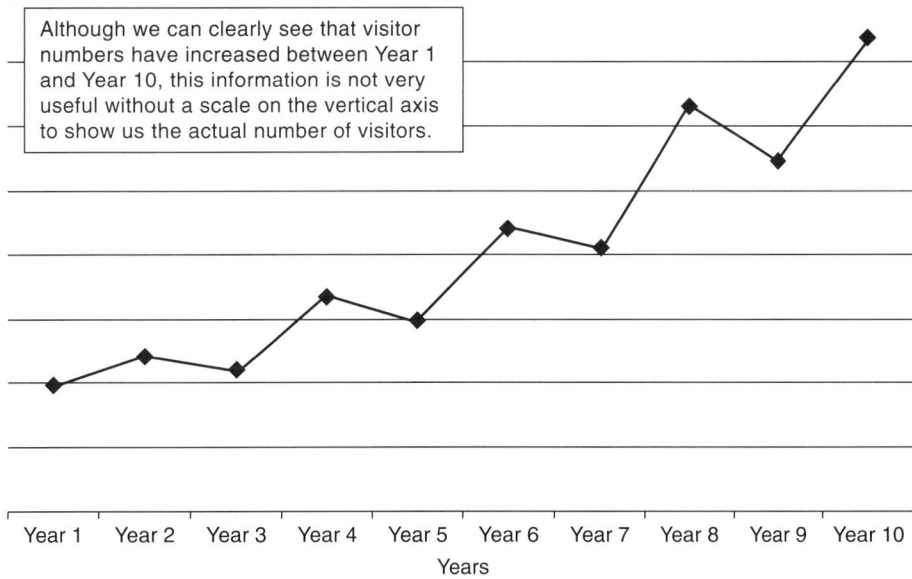

Although we can clearly see that visitor numbers have increased between Year 1 and Year 10, this information is not very useful without a scale on the vertical axis to show us the actual number of visitors.

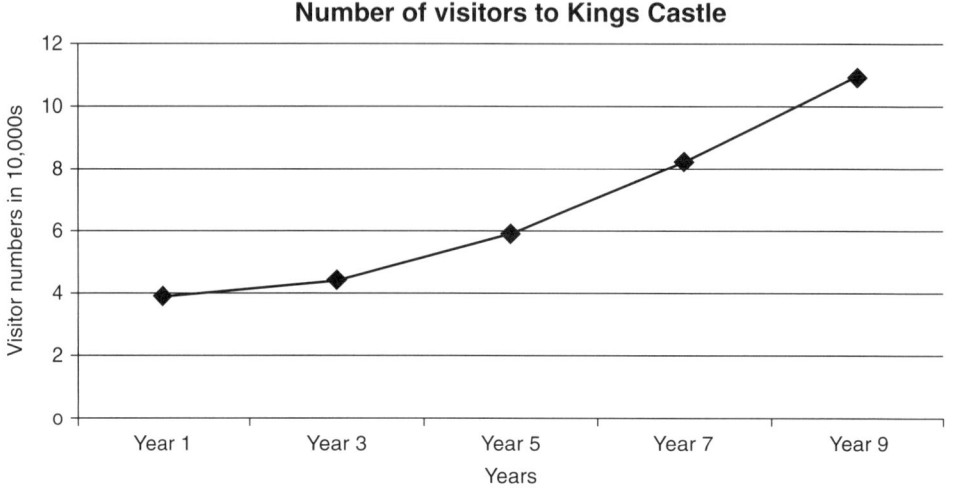

Number of visitors to Kings Castle

On this graph, the data points for some of the years are missing, making it look as though the visitor numbers have increased every year – we can see from the previous graph that this is not true.

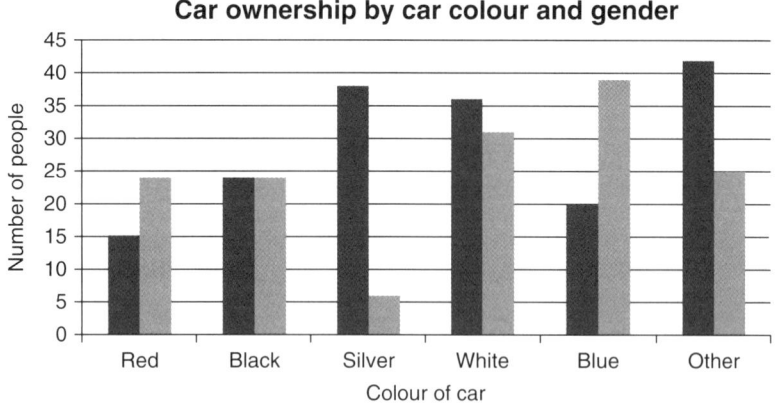

Car ownership by car colour and gender

This bar chart shows some potentially interesting information about the gender of car owners, but without a key, it is not possible to work out which bars relate to female owners and which represent males.

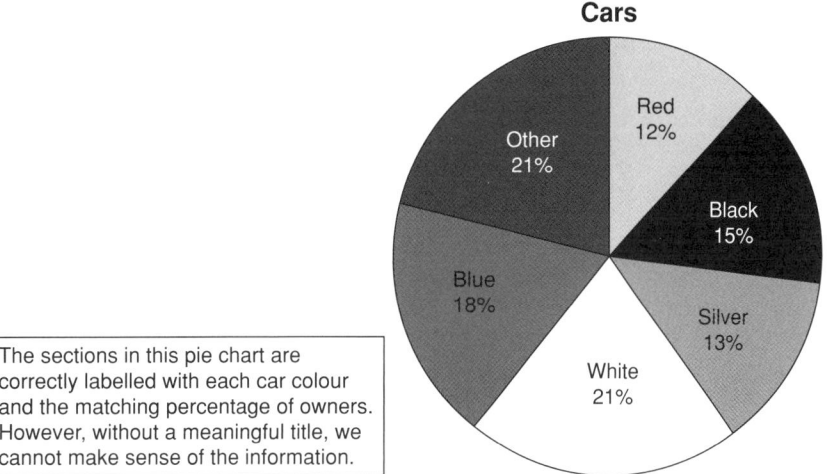

The sections in this pie chart are correctly labelled with each car colour and the matching percentage of owners. However, without a meaningful title, we cannot make sense of the information.

Choosing an appropriate and accurate scale for the vertical axis on a graph or chart is essential because the scale is used to read the data values and also allows us to make numerical comparisons. There are two important things to remember: make sure the scale starts at zero and choose the maximum value on your axis carefully.

Look at the carefully drawn graph below. The scale for the vertical axis is equally spaced and starts at zero. It has a sensible maximum value on the axis which is slightly larger than biggest data value.

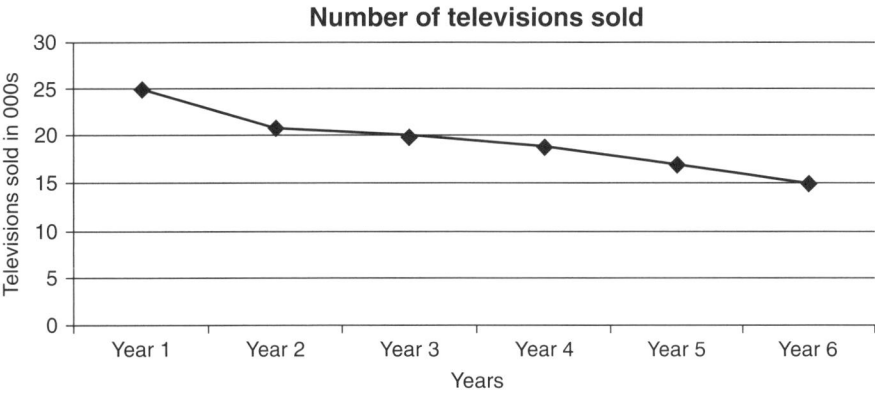

In contrast, the graph below shows the impact of using a misleading scale for the vertical axis.

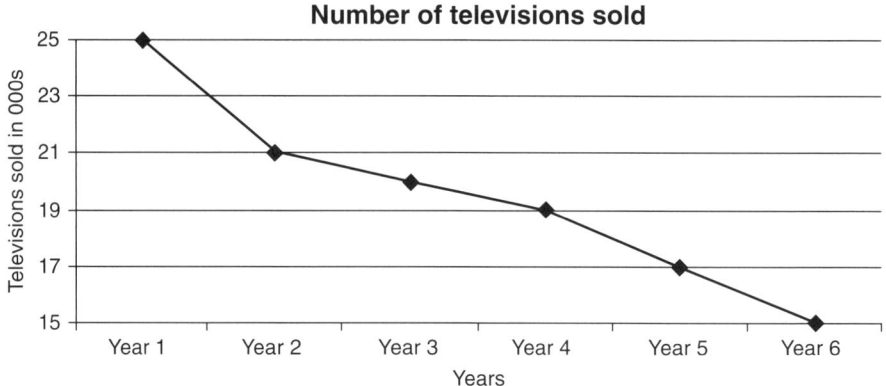

The minimum and maximum values on the vertical axis on this graph are the same as the smallest and largest data values. This makes the fall in television sales look much steeper and more dramatic.

Exercise 1

Describe two ways in which the three-dimensional pie chart on the left is misleading compared to the one on the right.

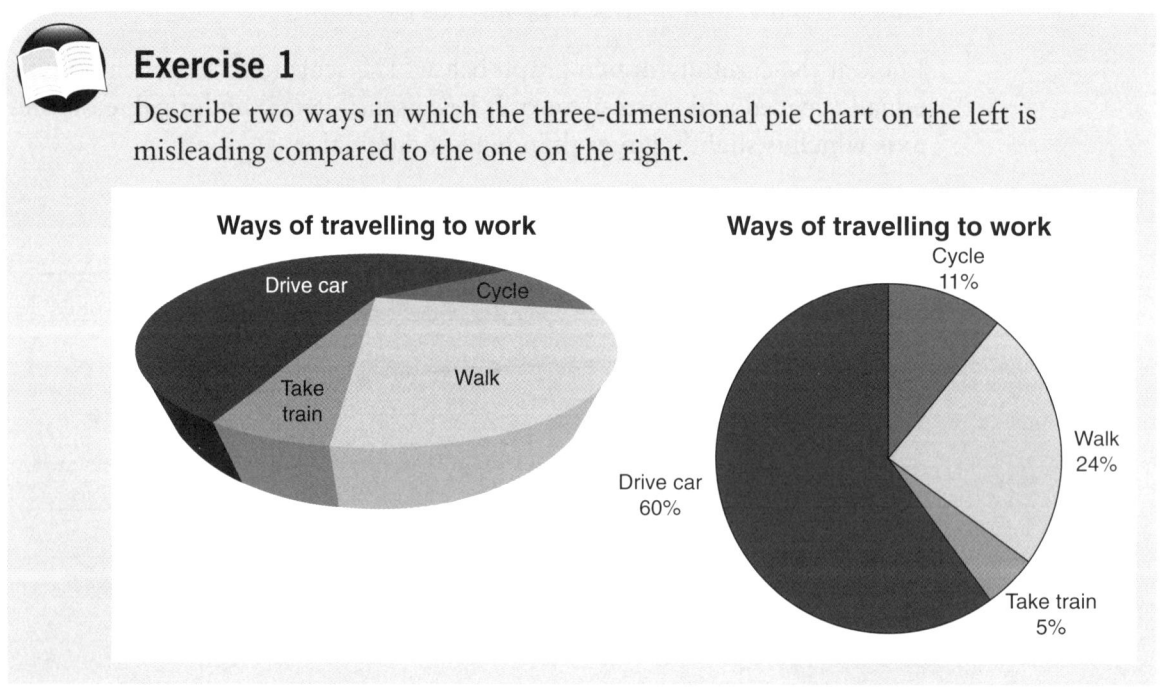

Exercise 2

To avoid creating a misleading graphic because of missing information, list four important details that should be included on every diagram.

The language of cause and effect

Along with correlations, it is important to be able to express cause and effect relationships accurately when dealing with data from research. These can be discussed using a range of conjunctions, verbs and nouns.

Conjunctions

We can use conjunctions such as:

as a result   *on account of*   *hence*

Many conjunctions can be positioned both at the start and in the middle of a sentence. For example:

- ***As a result of** the economic decline fewer house purchases were made.*

- *Fewer house purchases were made **as a result of** the economic decline.*

Other words are used more commonly at the start of a phrase or are marked with a semi-colon and a comma. For example:

- ***Consequently**, people are less willing to return to work.*

- *Salaries have fallen dramatically in recent years; **consequently,** people are less willing to return to work.*

Verbs and nouns

In addition to a range of conjunctions, a number of nouns and verbs can also be used to highlight a cause and effect relationship. For example:

- *The **impact** of less than four hours' sleep on concentration was investigated.*

- *The success of the project was **attributed** to the replication of the research environment.*

Exercise 3

Circle the cause and effect marker in each sentence. Then underline each cause and highlight each effect.

1   As a result of increased prices, people are continually making alternative purchases.

2   On account of bad weather, analysts claim up to $ 5billion is lost annually.

3   Adverse economic conditions have affected a range of commodities. Hence, prices have rapidly increased.

4   In the previous decade there has been a significant increase in the numbers of graduates worldwide. In part this is due to the expansion of university education in developing economies.

5   Many medical advances are actually made by companies. Therefore, diseases and conditions that are likely to generate a profit are targeted.

6   Fifteen questionnaires were spoiled or incomplete and consequently discarded from the analysis.

Exercise 4

Match each word on the left to its definition.

1	impact	a	the beginning, cause or source of something
2	factor	b	the way in which two or more people or things are connected with or involve each other
3	origin	c	the sudden and powerful effect that something has on a situation, process or person
4	to attribute	d	to be one of the causes of an event or situation
5	to contribute	e	to say something is caused by that event or action
6	relationship	f	to say a person or thing is responsible for something or that they caused it in a negative way
7	to blame	g	one of the things that affects an event, decision or situation

Exercise 5

Complete each sentence with a word from Exercise 4. You may need to change the form.

1   The one _____ that influences purchasing decisions more than any other is peers.

2   The _____ of social media on relationships in the home is strong.

3   Many people _____ previous generations for their inability to purchase a property.

4   The _____ of many people's feelings could be traced back to their own educational experiences.

5   The _____ between effort and results was not seen as clear cut in some countries.

6   The majority of respondents _____ their stress issues to multiple deadlines.

7   Significant life changes _____ towards stress levels rising.

For more information on language to discuss cause and effect, see Chapter 10.

Generalizations and specifics

When dealing with data we often choose to focus on specific interesting examples or to make generalizations from the data. When making generalizations, always remember to keep the sample size in mind and do not overgeneralize.

For example, if a study of motivation was conducted under the following conditions it would limit how we could generalize about the data:

A study of motivation

One company

One country

One state

Two professions – accountants and engineers

Conducted in the 1950s

However, it could be considered an overgeneralization to use the study conducted under the conditions listed to talk about motivation in these contexts:

Other companies

Other countries

Other states

Other professions

Different eras

Therefore, when interpreting our data we need to be careful to consider exactly what it shows and not to make any claims that overgeneralize it.

Exercise 6

Match the underlined expression in sentences 1–5 with the words in italics in sentences a–e.

1	There were a number of <u>small items of information</u> relevant to each respondent.	a	It is not logical to make broad *generalizations* from such a small sample set.
2	This section will <u>give a description without giving much detail of</u> the key findings of the study.	b	In the previous section the research method was *outlined*.
3	It is clearly a <u>general statement</u> to argue that gender impacts on educational attainment.	c	*In general*, assessment methods are as much about maintaining standards as they are about demonstrating academic achievement.
4	The <u>typical features</u> that many found attractive included the design and navigability.	d	One *characteristic* that stood out was the teacher's beliefs about discipline.
5	<u>Normally</u>, it is argued that examinations are more stressful than coursework.	e	The *details* of the piloting process can be found in Appendix B.

Presenting arguments

Much of academic writing looks at presenting arguments based on research. It is important when presenting an argument that you try to look at a range of perspectives to make the stance you take more informed.

For more information on language used to present supporting and alternative arguments, linking expressions, comparative structures, superlative structures and cautious language, see Chapters 10 and 11.

Exercise 7

Look at the sentences below and decide which ones:
a Present an additional argument that supports a previous one.
b Present an alternative or counter argument.

1   On the other hand, internet use is increasing on mobile devices.

2   However, little was done to find the company an alternative strategy.

3   Data storage is becoming increasingly centralized. Furthermore, cloud computing is reducing the need for individual hard drives.

4   Additionally, countries with a sophisticated internet network are more likely to have a stable economy.

5   Older generations are less inclined to shop online, whereas younger generations have few concerns.

6   Hard work is seen as the key to success. Moreover, few feel you can achieve anything of note without it.

Stance

The stance you take in your argument is essentially the opinion you have after being informed by a range of perspectives or a variety of evidence from research. You can indicate your stance using a range of adverbs to show the position you are taking. Different adverbs have a different range of functions.

For example:

certainly, typically, perhaps, likely, apparently

are all used to express a degree of certainty or doubt. Using stance adverbs to express a degree of doubt enables you to avoid overgeneralization and show modesty when making claims or giving your opinion. In this way, your writing will be more authoritative.

Other adverbs can be used to express evaluation or an assessment of something. For example:

largely, generally, mainly, hopefully

For more information on stance adverbs to add caution to your opinion, see Chapter 10.

Exercise 8

Complete the paragraph below using adverbs from the box. More than one adverb may be possible.

apparently	certainly	generally	largely	probably	typically

The research (1) _____ produced some interesting insights into people's decision-making processes. (2) _____, people are likely to take little time when the product is instantly consumable and of little value. (3) _____, products that are seen as being useful for at least five years involve a much longer and more detailed decision-making process.
(4) _____, according to most participants, value, durability and traditional design are the most important factors. This (5) _____ explains why a large proportion of participants are less influenced by brands in these cases. (6) _____, brands only came into consideration with the purchase of cars.

Evaluative language

All of the data you collect will need to be evaluated. Furthermore, when conducting a literature review or research for an essay you will also often need to evaluate many aspects of what you read. Bear in mind that it is not only the data that you will have to evaluate. All stages of the process need to be evaluated, whether you are looking at your own research or

Glossary

evaluate
If you evaluate
something or
someone, you
consider them in
order to make
a judgement
about them, for
example about
how good or bad
they are.

neutrality
If a person
shows neutrality,
they adopt a
position of not
supporting any
side in a debate
or evaluation.

that of someone else. This means you will have to evaluate the research method used, looking at things such as:

- The appropriateness of the technique used

- The quality of the questions

- The research environment

You will also need to look at other people's data and the conclusions they have drawn based on the data. For example, have they:

- Drawn reasonable conclusions based on the sample size?

- Considered the transferability to other contexts accurately?

- Under or overemphasized particular aspects?

- Considered all areas that may have influenced the data they have collected?

It is important to make sure that an evaluation looks at both positive and negative aspects and tries to maintain neutrality as much as possible.

Exercise 9

Look at the sentences below and decide whether each bold word is positive or negative in meaning.

1   The research process was **flawed** as it was virtually impossible to replicate.

2   Paulson's research in this area was **ground-breaking**.

3   This development was **crucial** to furthering the field.

4   His work was **seminal** in the field of genetics.

5   The sample size was **inadequate** to draw any valuable conclusions.

6   The **comprehensive** nature of the survey means that it provides detailed insights.

7   Arguably, the conclusions drawn are **mistaken** as they do not take income into consideration.

8   A **significant** finding was the impact of education on health.

Exercise 10

Use one of the words in the box to change the expressions in italics.

challenges	limited	notable	solid	underlined	validity

1   The *soundness* of the research was questionable.

2   The research process was *strong*.

3   One *unusual and interesting* finding concerned the variety of fruit eaten.

4   The findings *emphasized* the importance of the study.

5   The sample size was arguably *too small*.

6   There were a number of *difficulties* in maintaining consistency in replicating the experiment.

Reaching conclusions

Glossary

deduction
A deduction is a conclusion that you have reached about something because of other things that you know to be true.

Summarizing and concluding are a key part of academic writing. They highlight for the reader the key issues discussed in a piece of writing or discovered through a piece of research. In general, conclusions include a number of the following features:

- A summary of the main points

- A statement of your opinion or position based on the information presented

- A logical deduction based on the evidence presented

- A restatement of the thesis – in other words a restatement of the main aim or argument

- A future perspective; for example, which particular areas you feel need to be researched further

In general, conclusions do not present any new information that has not been discussed previously in the piece of writing.

Exercise 11

Complete each sentence with a word or phrase from the box.

attempted	balance	final	In brief	In conclusion

1   This study has _____ to look further into the impact of praise on motivation.

2   _____, to a certain extent this project has not found evidence to support the hypothesis proposed.

3   On _____, an alternative research method would have perhaps been more appropriate.

4   _____, the effort outweighed ability.

5   One _____ issue that needs further investigation is the socio-economic background and its impact.

Remember

✓ Survey results can and usually should be interpreted both visually and in writing.

✓ Choose the most appropriate graphic to accurately reflect your findings.

✓ Avoid producing misleading diagrams by checking that the visual perspective and scale on the vertical axis are correct and that all information is included.

✓ Do not claim a cause and effect relationship for something that is only correlated.

✓ Be cautious in any conclusions you draw. Do not generalize into areas too dissimilar from your sample, or generalize beyond what your sample size will allow.

✓ Clearly show your stance when presenting your own arguments.

✓ Evaluate all stages of the research process and not simply the results.

Further reading

Chapter 1

This book is excellent for working on your academic vocabulary in many different subject areas:
McCarthy, M., and O'Dell, F., *Academic Vocabulary in Use* (Cambridge: Cambridge University Press, 2008).

This book will give you further practice on many of the key topics related to statistics:
Rumsey, D., *Statistics for Dummies* (Indianapolis: Wiley Publishing, 2011).

If you want to practise academic vocabulary in the context of further reading then this book is ideal:
Schmitt, D., and Schmitt, N., *Focus on Vocabulary 2: Mastering the Academic Word List* (Harlow: Pearson, 2011).

This book is a good resource for both beginners and more experienced users of Microsoft Excel:
Harvey, G., *Excel 2010 for Dummies* (Indianapolis: Wiley Publishing, 2010).

An introductory book for Statistics including case studies from a variety of application areas:
Wood, M., *Making Sense of Statistics* (Hampshire: Palgrave Macmillan, 2003).

Chapter 2

This is useful as an introductory reading to some key areas in doing undergraduate research:
Wisker, G., The *Undergraduate Research Handbook* (London: Palgrave Macmillan, 2009).

This is useful as an introductory reading to some key areas in doing postgraduate research:
Wisker, G., *The Postgraduate Research Handbook* (London: Palgrave Macmillan, 2007).

There are many books that are specific to different subject fields. Here is a selection of some in a range of academic subject areas:
Allen, A., *Research Skills for Medical Students* (Exeter: Learning Matters, 2012).
Farrel, P., *Writing a Built Environment Dissertation: Practical Guidance and Examples* (Oxford: Wiley and Blackwell, 2010).
Halperin, S., and Heath, O., *Political Research: Methods and Practical Skills* (Oxford: Oxford University Press, 2012).
Sekaran, U., and Bougie, R., *Research Methods for Business: A Skill Building Approach* (5th edn, Indianapolis: John Wiley and Sons, 2009).
Sharp, J., *Success with your Education Research Project* (Exeter: Learning Matters, 2009).

Chapter 3

For a more detailed look at some of the research methods discussed in this chapter the following are some good resources:
Bryman, A., *Social Research Methods* (4th edn, Oxford: Oxford University Press, 2012).

Davies, M. B., *Doing a Successful Research Project: Using Qualitative or Quantitative Methods* (London: Palgrave Macmillan, 2007).

Kumar, R., *Research Methodology: A Step-by-Step Guide for Beginners* (3rd edn, London: Sage Publications, 2010).

Chapter 4

For further work on questionnaire design the following are a good reference:

Brink, T. L., *Questionnaires: Practical Hints on How to Avoid Mistakes in Design and Interpretation* (Chesterfield: Heuristic Books, 2004).

Gillham, B., *Developing a Questionnaire* (London: Continuum, 2000).

Chapter 5

For further work on interviews the following are a good reference:

King, N., and Horrocks, C., *Interviews in qualitative research* (London: Sage Publications, 2010).

Kvale, S., *InterViews: Learning the Craft of Qualitative Research Interviewing* (London: Sage Publications, 2008).

Chapters 6, 7 and 8

The following books provide a useful resource for learning some basic mathematical techniques including percentages and averages, as well as graphics:

Beveridge, C., *Basic Maths for Dummies* (West Sussex: Wiley Publishing, 2011).

Elwes, R., *The Maths Handbook: Everyday Maths Made Simple* (London: Quercus, 2011).

Graham, A., *Basic Mathematics* (London: Teach Yourself, 2010).

Graham, A., *Understanding Statistics* (London: Teach Yourself, 2010).

Lakin, S., *How to Improve your Maths Skills* (Harlow: Prentice Hall, 2011).

Chapters 9–12

For further reading on data analysis the following are a good reference:

Best, S., *Understanding and Doing Successful Research: Data Collection and Analysis for the Social Sciences* (Harlow: Pearson, 2012).

De Vaus, D., *Analyzing Social Science Data: 50 Key Problems in Data Analysis* (London: Sage Publications, 2002).

Silverman, D., *Interpreting Qualitative Data* (London: Sage Publications, 2011).

The grammar of fractions

There are a number of basic rules to remember when writing about fractions.

When you want to show how large a part of something is compared to the whole of it, you use a **fraction**, such as **a third** or **two-fifths**, followed by **of** and a noun phrase referring to the whole thing. Most fractions are based on ordinal numbers; the exceptions are **a half** and **a quarter**.

When referring to one part of something, you usually use **a**. You only use **one** in formal speech and writing or when you want to emphasize the amount.

*This state produces **a third** of the nation's oil.*

*... **one quarter** of the total population.*

Plural fractions are often written with a hyphen:

*More than **two-thirds** of the globe's surface is water.*

*He was not due at the office for another **three-quarters** of an hour.*

You can put an adjective in front of a fraction, after **the**:

*... **the southern** half of England.*

*... the first **two-thirds** of this century.*

When you use **a half** and **a quarter** in combination with whole numbers, they come in front of the plural noun you are using:

*... **one and a half** acres of land.*

*... **five and a quarter** days.*

However, if you are using **a** instead of the number **one**, the noun modified by **a** is singular and comes in front of the fraction word.

*... **an acre and a half** of land.*

Agreement of fractions

When you talk about a part of a single thing, you use a singular verb form:

*Two-fifths of the forest **was** removed.*

However, when you talk about part of a group of things, you use a plural form of the verb:

*A quarter of the students **were** seen individually.*

Fractions as pronouns

When it is clear who or what you are referring to, you can use fractions without **of** and a noun phrase:

*One fifth **are** appointed by the regional health authority.*

Materials taken from *Collins COBUILD English Usage*, 3rd edition, © HarperCollins Publishers 2012.

Glossary

Some of the more difficult words from the chapters are defined here in this Glossary. The definitions focus on the meanings of the words in the context in which they appear in the text. Definitions are from *COBUILD Advanced Dictionary*.

Key

ADJ	adjective	N-UNCOUNT	uncountable noun
ADV	adverb	N-VAR	variable noun
AUX	auxiliary verb	NEG	negative
COLOUR	colour word	NUM	number
COMB	combining form	ORD	ordinal
CONJ	conjunction	PASSIVE	see V-PASSIVE
CONVENTION	convention	PHRASAL VERB	phrasal verb
DET	determiner	PHRASE	phrase
EXCLAM	exclamation	PREDET	predeterminer
FRACTION	fraction	PREFIX	prefix
LINK	see V-LINK	PREP	preposition
MODAL	modal verb	PRON	pronoun
N-COUNT	countable noun	QUANT	quantifier
N-PLURAL	plural noun	QUEST	question word
N-PROPER	proper noun	SUFFIX	suffix
N-PROPER-PLURAL	plural proper noun	VERB	verb
N-SING	singular noun	V-LINK	link verb
N-TITLE	title noun	V-PASSIVE	passive verb

a

abundant ADJ
Something that is abundant is present in large quantities.

add up (adds up, adding up, added up) VERB
Add up means the same as add. If you add up numbers or amounts, you calculate their total.

aggregate ADJ
An aggregate amount or score is made up of several smaller amounts or scores added together.

allocate (allocates, allocating, allocated) VERB
If one item or share of something is allocated to a particular person or for a particular purpose, it is given to that person or used for that purpose.

ambiguous ADJ
If you describe something as ambiguous, you mean that it is unclear or confusing because it can be understood in more than one way.

archive (archives) N-COUNT
The archive or archives are a collection of documents and records that contain historical information. You can also use archives to refer to the place where archives are stored.

aspect (aspects) N-COUNT
Aspect is the way that a verb group shows whether an activity is continuing, is repeated, or is completed. For example, in 'They were laughing', the verb is in the progressive aspect and shows that the action was continuing.

attitude (attitudes) N-COUNT
Your attitude to something is the way that you think and feel about it, especially when this shows in the way you behave.

attribute (attributes) N-COUNT
An attribute is a quality or feature that someone or something has.

authoritative ADJ
Someone or something that is authoritative has a lot of knowledge of a particular subject.

authority N-UNCOUNT
If someone speaks or writes with authority, people respect and take notice of what they say because they have special knowledge of a subject.

auxiliary verb (auxiliary verbs) N-COUNT
An auxiliary verb is a verb which is used with a main verb, for example to form different tenses or to make the verb passive. In English, the basic auxiliary verbs are 'be', 'have', and 'do'. Modal verbs such as 'can' and 'will' are also sometimes called auxiliary verbs.

axis (axes) N-COUNT
An axis of a graph is one of the two lines on which the scales of measurement are marked.

b

band (bands) N-COUNT
A band is a range of numbers or values within a system of measurement.

bar chart (bar charts) N-COUNT
A bar chart is a graph which uses parallel rectangular shapes to represent changes in the size, value or rate of something or to compare the amount of something relating to a number of different countries or groups.

bias (biases) N-VAR
Bias is a tendency to prefer one person or thing to another, and to favour that person or thing.

biased ADJ
If someone is biased, they prefer one group of people to another, and behave unfairly as a result. You can also say that a process or system is biased.

brainstorm (brainstorms, brainstorming, brainstormed) VERB
If a group of people brainstorm, they have a meeting in which they all put forward as many ideas and suggestions as they can think of. This can also be done as an individual task.

c

capacity (capacities) N-VAR
The capacity of a container is its volume, or the amount of liquid it can hold, measured in units such as litres or gallons.

category (categories) N-COUNT
If people or things are divided into categories, they are divided into groups in such a way that the members of each group are similar to each other in some way.

cell (cells) N-COUNT
A cell is one of the small squares in a chart or spreadsheet into which you can add a single piece of data.

census (censuses) N-COUNT
A census is an official survey of the population of a country that is carried out in order to find out how many people live there and to obtain details of such things as people's ages and jobs.

characteristic (characteristics) N-COUNT
The characteristics of a person or thing are the qualities or features that belong to them and make them recognizable.

chart (charts) N-COUNT
A chart is a diagram, picture or graph which is intended to make information easier to understand.

class (classes) N-VAR
Class refers to the division of society into groups according to their social status.

cluster (clusters) N-COUNT
A cluster of people or things is a small group of them close together.

column (columns) N-COUNT
On a printed page such as a page of a dictionary, newspaper, or printed table or chart, a column is one of two or more vertical sections which are read downwards.

confidential ADJ
Information that is confidential is meant to be kept secret or private.

conjunctive adverb (conjunctive adverbs) N-COUNT
A conjunctive adverb is an adverb that connects two clauses, such as 'therefore' in 'The car had broken down; therefore we had to walk to school.'

constraint (constraints) N-COUNT
A constraint is something that limits or controls what you can do.

construct (constructs) N-COUNT
In the area of research, a construct is an idea, belief, or subject which is based on evidence which may not be true, and which you want to test and measure.

consumable ADJ
Consumable goods are items which are intended to be bought, used, and then replaced. Consumable is also a noun.

control group (control groups) N-COUNT
A control group is a group of subjects that is used as a comparison in order to check results in an experiment. The term is especially used of a group of patients who receive either a placebo (= substance with no effect) or a standard drug during an investigation of the effects of another drug on other patients.

co-ordinator (co-ordinators) N-COUNT
A co-ordinator is a word such as 'and', 'or', or 'but' which joins two or more words, groups, or clauses of equal status, for example two main clauses.

correlation (correlations) N-COUNT
A correlation between things is a connection or link between them.

cyclical ADJ
A cyclical process is one in which a series of events happens again and again in the same order.

d

daffodil (daffodils) N-COUNT
A daffodil is a yellow spring flower with a central part shaped like a tube and a long stem.

data N-UNCOUNT
You can refer to information as data, especially when it is in the form of facts or statistics that you can analyse. In American English, data is usually a plural noun. In technical or formal British English, data is sometimes a plural noun, but at other times, it is an uncountable noun.

deduction (deductions) N-COUNT
A deduction is a conclusion that you have reached about something because of other things that you know to be true.

denominator (denominators) N-COUNT
In mathematics, the denominator is the number which appears under the line in a fraction.

dependent clause (dependent clauses) N-COUNT
A dependent clause is a clause in a sentence which adds to or completes the information given in the main clause. It cannot usually stand alone as a sentence.

diagram (diagrams) N-COUNT
A diagram is a simple drawing which consists mainly of lines and is used, for example, to explain how a machine works.

digit (digits) N-COUNT
A digit is a written symbol for any of the ten numbers from 0 to 9.

disability (disabilities) N-COUNT
A disability is a permanent injury, illness, or physical or mental condition that tends to restrict the way that someone can live their life.

discrete ADJ
Discrete ideas or things are separate and distinct from each other.

display (displays, displaying, displayed) VERB
If you display something, you show it to people.

distort (distorts, distorting, distorted) VERB
If something you can see or hear is distorted or distorts, its appearance or sound is changed so that it seems unclear.

distribution (distributions) N-VAR
The distribution of something is how much of it there is in each place or at each time, or how much of it each person has.

dominant ADJ
Someone or something that is dominant is more powerful, successful, influential, or noticeable than other people or things.

dominate (dominates, dominating, dominated) VERB
To dominate a situation means to be the most powerful or important person or thing in it.

drift (drifts) N-COUNT
A drift is a movement away from somewhere or something, or a movement towards somewhere or something different.

drop-down menu (drop-down menus) N-COUNT
A drop-down menu is a list of options that appears on a computer screen when you select an item with a computer mouse.

durability N-UNCOUNT
Durability is the quality of something that is strong and lasts a long time without breaking or becoming weaker.

e

empirical ADJ
Empirical evidence or study relies on practical experience rather than theories.

equivalent ADJ
If one amount or value is equivalent to another, they are the same.

estimate (estimates, estimating, estimated) VERB
If you estimate a quantity or value, you make an approximate judgment or calculation of it.

ethical ADJ
If you describe something as ethical, you mean that it is morally right or morally acceptable.

ethnic ADJ
Ethnic means connected with or relating to different racial or cultural groups of people.

evaluate (evaluates, evaluating, evaluated) VERB
If you evaluate something or someone, you consider them in order to make a judgment about them, for example about how good or bad they are.

exaggerate (exaggerates, exaggerating, exaggerated) VERB
If you exaggerate, you indicate that something is, for example, worse or more important than it really is.

expenditure (expenditures) N-VAR
Expenditure is the spending of money on something, or the money that is spent on something.

experiment group (experiment groups) N-COUNT
An experiment group is a group of subjects that is exposed to the conditions of an experiment. The results from the experiment group are then compared with those from the control group.

expression (expressions) N-VAR
The expression of ideas or feelings is the showing of them through words, actions, or artistic activities.

extrinsic ADJ
Extrinsic reasons, forces, or factors exist outside the person or situation they affect.

f

facilitate (facilitates, facilitating, facilitated) VERB
To facilitate an action or process, especially one that you would like to happen, means to make it easier or more likely to happen.

facilitator (facilitators) N-COUNT
A facilitator is a person or organization that helps another person or organization to do or to achieve a particular thing.

feature (features) N-COUNT
A feature of something is an interesting or important part or characteristic of it.

flimsy ADJ
If you describe something such as evidence or an excuse as flimsy, you mean that it is not very good or convincing.

formula (formulae or formulas) N-COUNT
A formula is a group of letters, numbers, or other symbols which represents a scientific or mathematical rule.

g

gender (genders) N-VAR
A person's gender is the fact that they are male or female.

generalized ADJ
Generalized means involving many different things rather than one or two specific things.

graphic (graphics) N-COUNT
Graphics are drawings and pictures that are composed using simple lines and sometimes strong colours.

grid (grids) N-COUNT
A grid is something which is in a pattern of straight lines that cross over each other, forming squares. On maps the grid is used to help you find a particular thing or place.

h

hedging ADJ
Hedging language is language which you use to avoid answering a question or committing yourself to a particular opinion or decision.

hence ADV
You use hence to indicate that the statement you are about to make is a consequence of what you have just said.

horizontally ADV
If something is positioned or moves horizontally, it is in a position or moves in a direction that is flat and level with the ground rather than at an angle to it.

hypothesis (hypotheses) N-COUNT
A hypothesis is an idea which is suggested as a
possible explanation for a particular situation or
condition, but which has not yet been proved to
be correct.

i

impact (impacts) N-COUNT
The impact that something has on a situation,
process or person is a sudden and powerful effect
that it has on them.

incentive (incentives) N-COUNT
If something is an incentive to do something, it
encourages you to do it.

independent clause (independent clauses) N-COUNT
An independent clause is a clause that
contains a subject and a verb, expresses a
complete thought, and can stand alone as a
sentence.

influence (influences, influencing, influenced) VERB
If you influence someone, you use your
power to make them agree with you or do what
you want.

intensity (intensities) N-VAR
The intensity of something is how great or extreme
it is in strength or degree.

interpret (interprets, interpreting, interpreted) VERB
If you interpret something in a particular way, you
decide that this is its meaning or significance.

intersection (intersections) N-COUNT
An intersection is a place where lines or roads meet
or cross.

interviewee (interviewees) N-COUNT
An interviewee is a person who is being
interviewed.

intrinsic ADJ
If something has intrinsic value or intrinsic interest,
it is valuable or interesting because of its basic
nature or character, and not because of its
connection with other things.

isolate (isolates, isolating, isolated) VERB
If you isolate something such as an idea or a
problem, you separate it from others that it is
connected with, so that you can concentrate on it
or consider it on its own.

j

journal (journals) N-COUNT
A journal is an account which you write of your
daily activities.

k

key (keys) N-COUNT
The key on a map or diagram or in a technical
book is a list of the symbols or abbreviations
used and their meanings.

key ADJ
A key issue, area, or part of something is the most
important issue, area, or part.

l

label (labels, labelling, labelled) VERB
If something is labelled, a label is attached to it
giving information about it.

leading question (leading questions) N-COUNT
A leading question is expressed in such a way that
it suggests what the answer should be.

liberal ADJ
Someone who has liberal views believes people
should have a lot of freedom in deciding how to
behave and think.

line graph (line graphs) N-COUNT
A line graph is a graph which uses lines connecting
points to show changes in the value of something.

m

marital status N-UNCOUNT
Your marital status is whether you are married,
single, or divorced.

mass (masses) N-VAR
In physics, the mass of an object is the amount of
physical matter that it has.

mean N-SING
The mean is a number that is the average of a set of
numbers.

median ADJ
The median value of a set of values is the middle
one when they are arranged in order. For
example, if a group of five students take a test
and their marks are 5, 7, 7, 8, and 10, the median
mark is 7.

method (methods) N-COUNT
A method is a particular way of doing something.

misinterpret (misinterprets, misinterpreting, misinterpreted) VERB
If you misinterpret something, you understand it wrongly.

misleading ADJ
If you describe something as misleading, you mean that it gives you a wrong idea or impression.

misread (misreads, misreading, misread) VERB
If you misread something that has been written or printed, you look at it and think that it says something that it does not say.

mode N-SING
The mode is a value that occurs most frequently in a set of values.

modesty N-UNCOUNT
If you write with modesty, you use impersonal and cautious language in your writing.

n

neutrality N-UNCOUNT
If a person shows neutrality, they adopt a position of not supporting any side in a debate or evaluation.

numerator (numerators) N-COUNT
In mathematics, the numerator is the number which appears above the line in a fraction.

o

objectively ADV
If you look at something objectively, you base your opinions on facts rather than on your personal feelings.

omit (omits, omitting, omitted) VERB
If you omit something, you do not include it in an activity or piece of work, deliberately or accidentally.

on account of PHRASE
You use on account of to introduce the reason or explanation for something.

overlap (overlaps, overlapping, overlapped) VERB
If one idea or activity overlaps with another, they involve some of the same subjects, people, or periods of time.

p

participant (participants) N-COUNT
The participants in an activity are the people who take part in it.

perspective N-UNCOUNT
Perspective is the art of making some objects or people in a picture look further away than others.

pie chart (pie charts) N-COUNT
A pie chart is a circle divided into sections to show the relative proportions of a set of things.

pilot (pilots, piloting, piloted) VERB
If a government or organization pilots a programme or a scheme, they test it, before deciding whether to introduce it on a larger scale.

population (populations) N-COUNT
If you refer to a particular type of population in a country or area, you are referring to all the people or animals of that type there.

pop-up image (pop-up images) N-COUNT
A pop-up image is a small window containing a picture that appears on a computer screen when you perform a particular operation.

pre-coded ADJ
If a question or questionnaire is pre-coded, the person answering it is given a limited choice of options for their answers.

present (presents, presenting, presented) VERB
When you present information, you give it to people in a formal way.

primary sector (primary sectors) N-COUNT
The primary sector is the sector of an economy which makes direct use of natural resources, for example, agriculture, forestry and fishing, mining, etc.

proportion (proportions) N-COUNT
A proportion of a group or an amount is a part of it.

q

questionnaire (questionnaires) N-COUNT
A questionnaire is a written list of questions which are answered by a lot of people in order to provide information for a report or a survey.

quota (quotas) N-COUNT
A quota is the limited number or quantity of something which is officially allowed.

r

random ADJ
A random sample or method is one in which all the people or things involved have an equal chance of being chosen.

recruit (recruits, recruiting, recruited) VERB
If you recruit people for an organization, you select them and persuade them to join it or work for it.

reflection (reflections) N-VAR
Reflection is careful thought about a particular subject. Your reflections are your thoughts about a particular subject.

reluctant ADJ
If you are reluctant to do something, you are unwilling to do it and hesitate before doing it, or do it slowly and without enthusiasm.

replication N-UNCOUNT
Replication is the act of doing someone's experiment, work or research in exactly the same way as they did it.

respondent (respondents) N-COUNT
A respondent is a person who replies to something such as a survey or set of questions.

rotate (rotates, rotating, rotated) VERB
When something rotates or when you rotate it, it turns with a circular movement.

round up/down PHRASAL VERB
If you round an amount up or down, you change it to the nearest whole number or the nearest multiple of 10, 100, 1,000, and so on.

row (rows) N-COUNT
A row of things or people is a number of them arranged in a straight line.

s

sample (samples) N-COUNT
A sample of people or things is a number of them chosen out of a larger group and then used in tests or surveys, or used to provide information about the whole group.

sampling N-UNCOUNT
Sampling is the act of choosing a number of people or things out of a larger group to use in tests or surveys, or to provide information about the whole group.

scale (scales) N-COUNT
A scale is a set of levels or numbers which are used in a particular system of measuring things or are used when comparing things.

secondary sector (secondary sectors) N-COUNT
The secondary sector is the sector of the economy that creates finished products, for example, production and construction.

segment (segments) N-COUNT
A segment of a circle or pie chart is one of the parts into which it is divided when you draw straight lines through it.

set of data (sets of data) N-COUNT
A set of data is a number of facts that belong together or that are thought of as a group.

shading N-UNCOUNT
If you use shading on a chart, you colour an area darker than the surrounding areas, so that it can be distinguished from them.

specific ADJ
If someone is specific, they give a description that is precise and exact.

stance (stances) N-COUNT
Your stance on a particular matter is your attitude to it.

subordinator (subordinators) N-COUNT
A subordinator is a word such as 'although', 'because', or 'when' which begins a subordinate clause.

superlative ADJ
The superlative form of an adjective or adverb is the form that indicates that something has more of a quality than anything else in a group. For example, 'biggest' is the superlative form of 'big'.

t

table (tables) N-COUNT
A table is a written set of facts and figures arranged in columns and rows.

technique (techniques) N-COUNT
A technique is a particular method of doing an activity, usually a method that involves practical skills.

tertiary sector (tertiary sectors) N-COUNT
The tertiary sector is the service sector of an economy.

three-dimensional ADJ
A three-dimensional object is solid rather than flat, because it can be measured in three different directions, usually the height, length and width. The abbreviation 3-D can also be used.

transcribe (transcribes, transcribing, transcribed) VERB
If you transcribe a speech or text, you write it out in a different form from the one in which it exists, for example by writing it out in full from notes or from an audio recording.

trend (trends) N-COUNT
A trend is a change or development towards something new or different.

u

unique ADJ
Something that is unique is the only one of its kind.

unrepresentative ADJ
If you describe a group of people as unrepresentative, you mean that their views are not typical of the community or society to which they belong.

v

value (values) N-COUNT
In mathematics, the value of a symbol or letter is the amount represented by it.

variable (variables) N-COUNT
A variable is a factor that can change in quality, quantity, or size, which you have to take into account in a situation.

vertically ADV
If something is positioned or moves vertically, it is in a position or moves in a direction that is standing or pointing straight up.

visual ADJ
Visual means relating to sight, or to things that you can see.

w

whereas CONJ
You use whereas to introduce a comment which contrasts with what is said in the main clause.

while CONJ
You use while at the beginning of a clause to introduce information which contrasts with information in the main clause.

Answer key

Chapter 1

Exercise 1
Correct matched pairs are:

Unit of measurement	Item being measured
degrees Celsius (°C)	temperature of a cup of coffee
kilometres (km)	distance between London and Paris
kilometres per hour (km/h)	speed of a train
seconds (sec)	time taken to count to ten
millilitres (ml)	amount of orange juice in a glass
grams (g)	weight of a pencil

Exercise 2
1 aggregate / total

2 capacity

3 estimated

4 approximately

5 rounds up / down

6 maximum / minimum

7 mass

8 Accurate

Exercise 3
1 fraction

2 calculation

3 percentage

4 measurement

Exercise 4
1 estimation/estimate

2 calculate

3 approximately

4 addition

5 totalled

6 accurately

Exercise 5
Answers will vary.

Exercise 6
1 d   2 b   3 a   4 c

Exercise 7
1 quantitative

2 qualitative

3 qualitative

4 quantitative

5 quantitative

Exercise 8
1 A quantitative variable can be written down using numbers; a qualitative variable cannot be written down using numbers.

2 Answers will vary.
Examples: 15 (people on a bus), green (a green apple)

3 'type of tree' is qualitative because the observations are not numerical, for example: oak, sycamore. 'number of pupils in a class' is quantitative because the observations are numerical, for example: 32, 160.

Exercise 9
3, 1, 4, 2

Exercise 10
1 data

2 method

3 technique

4 patterns / features

5 sets of data

6 present / display

Exercise 11

collection – 1, 2

organization – 3, 4

interpreting – 5

presenting – 6

Exercise 12

1 a Business and Management

b 67%

2 a B5

b A2

Exercise 13

Pie chart

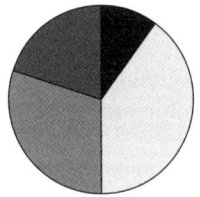

Bar chart

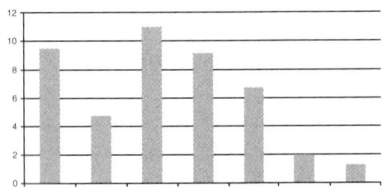

Line graph

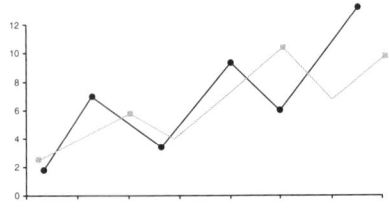

Table

Report

Month	Expence	Subtotal
Jan		
Feb		
March		
April		
May		
June		
Total		

Diagram

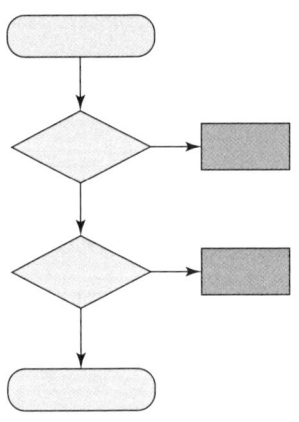

Exercise 14

1 horizontally / vertically

2 column / row

3 key / label / pie chart / line graph / axes

4 segments / pie chart

5 figures / charts

6 proportion / trends

Exercise 15

1 As is shown

2 in

3 graph 2.3

4 It can be seen from

Exercise 16

1 e   2 a   3 b   4 c   5 d

Chapter 2

Exercise 1
Answers will vary.

Exercise 2
Questions 1 and 2 are more focused than 3 and 4.

Exercise 3
Answers will vary.

Exercise 4
1 False

2 False

3 True

4 False

5 True

Exercise 5

Investigation	Sample population	Census: practical or impractical?
1 Finding out how many hours of homework are completed each week by the pupils in a specific class in a school.	The population is all of the pupils in a specific class – a census would be practical.	practical
2 Finding out the number of pets that are owned by adults in London.	The population is all of the adults in London – a census would be impractical.	impractical
3 Finding out the number of pages in each book in a large library.	The population is all of the books in a large library – a census would be impractical.	impractical
4 Finding out how many children in the UK walk to school in the morning.	The population is all of the children in the UK – a census would be impractical.	impractical

Avoiding bias
Football team investigation: the men at this football match are most likely to be supporters of Manchester City or Manchester United and so their favourite football team will not be representative of men who live in other cities around the UK and support their local football teams.

Car driving investigation: people who have just driven into the company car park are likely to think that this is the best way for them to travel to work; using an unbiased sample would involve choosing people who had arrived at work using different forms of transport.

Exercise 6
1 c   2 f   3 a   4 b   5 i   6 h   7 g
8 d   9 e

Exercise 7
1 representative

2 sampling

3 carried out

4 investigate

5 biased

6 estimated

7 census

8 population

9 draw / conclusion

Exercise 8
A hypothesis is something that you wish to test as part of your research. Largely, it involves looking at cause and effect relationships and trying to discover if they are true or not.

Exercise 9
Possible answers:

Low income is the main reason for job dissatisfaction.

2 What factors affect job satisfaction?

3 How important is income in determining job satisfaction?

4 Can other forms of payment such as commission and bonuses compensate for a low salary?

5 Do other factors such as praise negate the effect of low income?

6 Does it depend on the profession?

Blueberries have a positive impact on the mind.

2 What foods have a negative impact on the mind?

3 Do any other foods that have a positive effect have similarities with blueberries?

4 What is the chemical make-up of blueberries? What effect do these chemicals have?

Exercise 10
1, 2, 3

Exercise 11
1 Travelling abroad increases the risk of catching malaria.

2 Recycling can save money.

3 Low temperatures can lead to car accidents.

4 Language learning can increase cultural awareness.

Chapter 3

Exercise 1
Advantages: 1, 5, 6, 8, 9

Disadvantages: 2, 3, 4, 7

Exercise 2
1 during	5 before
2 before	6 during
3 during	7 before
4 after	8 before

Exercise 3
Possible answers:

- Focus groups can quickly become influenced by one or two dominant people.

- An inexperienced moderator may influence the discussion too much or allow people to dominate.

- Depending on the topic it can be difficult to have the participants share their real feelings towards something.

- Time and geographical constraints can make the method more unrepresentative compared to a questionnaire.

- The environment is quite unnatural and the fact that people know they are being watched and recorded may affect the quality of research results.

Exercise 4
(d) = dependent

(i) = independent

Variable 1	Variable 2
amount of time spent on revision (i)	score in a test (d)
number of ice creams sold (d)	temperature (i)
number of colds suffered in a year (d)	amount of fruit eaten each week (i)
heart rate (d)	running speed (i)
plant height (d)	amount of water given to a plant (i)
price of laptop (i)	number of laptops sold (d)

Exercise 5
You could conduct an experiment, prescribing a particularly healthy diet to people and then assessing any improvements in the level of fitness through repeated exercise routines.

Exercise 6

1 observation

2 questionnaire

3 questionaire

4 experiment

Chapter 4

Exercise 1

1 closed	4 open
2 closed	5 closed
3 open	6 open

Exercise 2

1 Have you ever seen *Citizen Kane*?

2 In your opinion, how would you rate the speed of your work?
In your opinion, how would you rate the quality of your work?

3 This question might be better as an open question or alternatively the list needs to include more items, e.g. food, clothing, etc. If this was a list question it would also need to be carefully piloted.

4 Where do you get most of your information about health?

Exercise 3

1 Could you spare a few moments?

2 Would you mind taking part in my survey?

3 Could I ask how old you are?

4 I was wondering if you had time to answer a few questions?

5 Can I ask what your profession is?

6 I'd like to take a few minutes to ask you some questions if possible?

Exercise 4

Opportunity sampling involves asking people who are willing or available to fill in your questionnaire or be interviewed.

Quota sampling involves categorizing the people in your population and then choosing to include in your sample a certain number of people from each group.

Exercise 5

For example, it would be appropriate to use random sampling in an investigation to find out how many hours of homework the pupils in a specific school work on each week during term-time; the population would be all of the pupils in the school.

Exercise 6

1 quota sampling

2 opportunity sampling

3 cluster sampling

Exercise 7

Advantages:

- costs for the use of online questionnaires can be lower because no photocopying, postage or stationery costs are involved

- a survey created using a computer program can look more interesting and use features such as pop-up images and drop-down menus

- responses received using online questionnaires can be processed electronically by being input directly into a spreadsheet or other type of computer package

Disadvantages:

- someone receiving the questionnaire can easily delete the email containing the request, thinking it is junk mail

- creating an online survey can be much more time-consuming than producing a paper version because it will be necessary to use a specialist software program

- technical problems may occur with an online questionnaire, preventing the people from filling it out or returning it

Exercise 8

You could offer entry into a prize draw to receive a new electronic gadget such as an e-reader, or you could offer a discount on books bought at the campus bookstore.

Exercise 9

Use a pilot study to test your questionnaire on a small group of people, such as friends or family members who will give their opinions on the questions honestly.

Chapter 5

Exercise 1

1 interviewee knowledge

2 past events

3 opinions and beliefs

4 general facts

5 general facts / interviewee knowledge

6 feelings

7 opinions and beliefs

8 past events

Exercise 2

1 How do you feel about your relationship with your siblings?

2 What do you think makes people happy?

3 How do you feel about branded clothing?

4 Where do you live?

5 Which of these do you value more?

6 Who is the leader of the UN?

7 Where did you go on holiday last year?

8 What is the role of charities?

Exercise 3

2 Would you shop online again?

3 Did you enjoy your stay in the hotel?

4 Do you ever travel to work by train?

5 Have you ever been camping?

6 Are you free to answer some questions?

7 Do you exercise every day?

Exercise 4

1 Who was

2 How often are

3 How did

4 What do / did

5 Where do / did

6 How long do / How many hours do

7 How often do

8 How much did

Exercise 5

1 object   2 object   3 object   4 subject
5 object   6 subject

Exercise 6

1 What did you choose that course for?

2 What kind of holidays are you interested in?

3 Which countries have you lived in?

4 What's the weather like where you live?

5 What you most commonly complain about?

6 Who do you live with?

Exercise 7

1 The interviewer/ee might have opinions about different age groups that affect their answers. For example, these opinions might affect how comfortable the interviewer/ee feels about talking about certain topics with someone from a different generation.

2 Certain topics might be affected by different genders or ethnic backgrounds, especially if there are opinions or beliefs related to the different groups being discussed.

3 If you are much more qualified it might make the person being interviewed more closed in their response.

Exercise 8

1 c   2 h   3 a   4 e   5 b   6 d
7 f   8 i

Exercise 9

2 indicate

3 show

4 notes

5 predict

6 reveals

7 supposes

Exercise 10

2 The organization predicts that fish stocks will decline.

3 Jackson (2012) shows the importance of a low fat diet.

4 Tse's findings confirm the findings from a previous study.

5 The study reveals previously unknown opinions.

Chapter 6

Exercise 1

1 62% of the people in the waiting room will be female.

2 54% of the revenue is profit.

Exercise 2

Answers will vary.

Exercise 3

1 £180

2 279 g

3 156 m

Exercise 4

1 10% = £25, so 30% = 3 × 10% = 3 × £25 = £75

2 10% = 8 kg, so 50% = 5 × 10% = 5 × 8 kg = 40 kg

3 10% = 34 cm, so 80% = 8 × 10% = 272 cm and 5% = 10% ÷ 2 = 17 cm, so 85% = 289 cm

Exercise 5

The box contains:

9 orange dreams

63 fudge delights

36 nutty clusters

27 coffee swirls

45 caramel moments

Exercise 6

1 15% of £44 = £6.60, so the sale price is £44 − £6.60 = £37.40

2 2% of £45,000 = £900, so her new earnings are £45,000 + £900 = £45,900

3 5% of £4.20 = 21p, so the new call charge is £4.20 + 21p = £4.41

Exercise 7

Verb	Noun
increase	increase
reduce	reduction
allocate	allocation
divide	division
multiply	multiplication
rise	rise
calculate	calculation

Exercise 8

1 increase

2 decreased

3 allocated

4 division

5 Multiply

6 rose

7 calculation

Exercise 9

1 $\frac{16}{6}$ is equal to c) $2\frac{4}{6}$

2 $4\frac{3}{4}$ is equal to b) $\frac{19}{4}$

Exercise 10

$\frac{4}{5} = \frac{24}{30}$, so the missing number is 24

Exercise 11

$\frac{5}{9}$ and $\frac{20}{36}$ are equivalent because $5 \times 4 = 20$ and

$9 \times 4 = 36$

Exercise 12

1 $\frac{2}{9}$ of 27 = 27 ÷ 9 × 2 = 3 × 2 = 6

2 $\frac{3}{5}$ of 55 = 55 ÷ 5 × 3 = 11 × 3 = 33

3 $\frac{4}{7}$ of 35 = 35 ÷ 7 × 4 = 5 × 4 = 20

Exercise 13

1 $\frac{6}{20}$ = 30%

2 $\frac{3}{25}$ = 12%

3 $\frac{8}{10}$ = 80%

4 $\frac{17}{50}$ = 34%

Exercise 14

1 78% = $\frac{78}{100}$ = $\frac{39}{50}$

2 30% = $\frac{30}{100}$ = $\frac{3}{10}$

3 85% = $\frac{85}{100}$ = $\frac{17}{20}$

4 44% = $\frac{44}{100}$ = $\frac{11}{25}$

Exercise 15

Fraction	$\frac{1}{2}$	$\frac{13}{50}$	$\frac{7}{20}$	$\frac{2}{5}$	$\frac{11}{25}$	$\frac{3}{100}$	$\frac{9}{50}$	$\frac{13}{20}$
Percentage	50%	26%	35%	40%	44%	3%	18%	65%

Exercise 16

1 $\frac{8}{25}$ is equal to 32%

2 $\frac{7}{10}$ is greater than 50%

3 $\frac{1}{4}$ is less than 30%

4 $\frac{18}{50}$ is equal to 36%

Exercise 17

for	from	to	with
account	benefit	attribute	associate
argue	decrease	compare	compare
	exclude	decrease	contrast
	increase	increase	provide
	rise	rise	

Exercise 18

2 accounted for

3 excluded from

4 attributed to

5 associated … with

6 decreased to

7 contrasts / contrasted with

8 provide … with

Exercise 19

1 b argument

2 a associate

3 a attribute

4 a benefit

5 b exclusion

6 b provision

7 a rise

8 b comparison

Exercise 20

2 The argument *with* the conclusion was that little evidence could be found to support the hypothesis.

3 Effort was seen as an important attribute *of* success in sport.

4 The benefits *of* increased exercise are numerous.

5 The exclusion *of* all fats in a diet is detrimental to health.

6 The provision *of* the right working conditions can increase staff productivity.

7 An increase *of* 12 per cent was seen.

8 A decrease *of* two fifths was found to have a significant impact.

Chapter 7

Exercise 1

1 The average annual income in the United States is $30,000.

2 The average score of the students was 68%.

3 The average number of calories consumed was 2,200.

4 The average weight of the participants was 84 kilos.

5 The average saving was £30 per person.

6 The average fall in house prices has been $20,000.

Exercise 2

1 False

2 True

3 False

4 True

5 False

Exercise 3

The mode is 230, which occurs twice.

The median is ½ (230 + 240) = 235

The mean is 1,930 ÷ 8 = 241.25

Exercise 4

1 Median because of the extreme value, 18.5.

2 Mode because the data is non-numeric.

3 Mean because it uses all of the data values in the calculation.

Exercise 5

1 b   2 c   3 a   4 g   5 e   6 f   7 d

Exercise 6

1 On average, respondents spent 30 minutes a day reading books, whereas they spent three hours a day on the internet.

2 On average, a graduate salary in Scotland is £30,000, while a non-graduate salary is only £25,000.

3 On average, the over-sixties spend £500 on internet shopping per year, in comparison to 25-35-year-olds, who spend £2,000.

4 On average, people spent £2,000 on holidays in 2011, compared to 2012, when people spent £3,000.

Exercise 7

The mode is 1 day, which occurs 15 times.

The mean is 40 ÷ 31 = 1.29 days

The median is 1 day, which is the 16th data value.

Exercise 8

1 Mode because the data is non-numeric.

2 Median because of the extreme value, 96.

3 Mean because it uses all of the data values in the calculation.

Chapter 8

Exercise 1

1 represents

2 illustrates

3 walk

4 take

5 don't drive / doesn't allow

Exercise 2
1 shows / illustrates

2 surf / search / access

3 use

4 look

5 download

6 phone

7 send

Exercise 3
1 were

2 visited

3 was

4 doubled

5 increased

6 went

Exercise 4
1 was

2 went

3 were

4 were

Exercise 5
1 have been

2 peaked

3 was / wasn't

4 have gone

5 have just had

6 caused

Exercise 6
1 has been

2 was

3 fell

4 decreased

5 was

Exercise 7
1 were questioned

2 was spent

3 was spent

4 were bought

5 spent

6 cost

7 spent

8 was spent

Exercise 8
1 are / were positively correlated

2 are / were sold

3 travelled

4 are / were

5 scored

6 achieve

Exercise 9
1 The passive is used in sentences 1, 3, 4, 6.

  The active is used in sentences 2 and 5.

2 In sentences 2 and 5 the focus is on the team, whereas in the other sentences the focus changes to describe what happened.

Exercise 10
1 All the verbs are in the past simple apart from the first sentence, where the verb is in the present simple passive.

2 The first sentence describes a situation that is true now, whereas the other sentences describe the outcome of a past event.

Exercise 11

Ages of brothers and sisters: this graphic should not be used because a pie chart shows the proportion of something as a whole; it does not make sense to talk about the age of an individual sibling as a percentage of the total ages of all siblings; we would usually choose to display this information in a table.

How students spend their money: this graphic is a line graph, which would normally be used to show the way in which something changes over time; this data is focused on the proportion of money spent on different categories rather than how student expenditure changes over time; it would be more appropriate to use a pie chart to display this information.

Daily hours of sunshine: it would be better to present this data as a line graph or a bar chart to show the differences in the daily hours of sunshine over the months we are interested in; a pictogram is the wrong type of graphic for this information because it would be very difficult to accurately show, for example, two hours of sunshine, using a fraction of a picture that represents eight hours in the key.

Exercise 12

1 The graphic **illustrates** the most common purchases in the shop each month.

2 Sales **increased** dramatically at the start of last year.

3 The website **has had** an increasing number of hits every month this year.

4 The most common way to travel to work last month **was** by car.

5 More drinks **were bought** in May than in June.

6 Brazil **exported** more coffee than any other nation last year.

7 The Chinese economy **grew** by 8% last year.

8 Buses **are used** every day by more students than any other group.

Chapter 9

Exercise 1

The graph shows an increase in unemployed school leavers in every quarter 3, which represents the summer period.

Exercise 2

There is an overall increasing trend in the number of visitors to the theme park in Spain.

Exercise 3

1 make different: modify, distort

2 less: decrease, diminish

3 more: increase, rise

4 bring together: incorporate, include

Exercise 4

1 will increase

2 distorted

3 decreased / diminished

4 modified

5 included / incorporated

6 included / incorporated

7 rose / increased

8 decreased / diminished

Exercise 5

Large difference	Small difference
considerably	marginally
dramatically	slightly
noticeably	somewhat
sharply	steadily
significantly	to a small degree

Numbers

Exercise 6
1 Country 1
2 Country 3
3 Country 3
4 Country 2
5 Country 1
6 Country 3
7 Country 2
8 Country 1
9 Country 3
10 Country 2

Exercise 7
Other answers are possible. You just need to make sure your verb indicates the right direction, up or down, and that your adverb reflects by how much it goes up or down.

1 rose significantly
2 increased slightly
3 fell marginally
4 went up considerably
5 decreased marginally
6 increased steadily

Exercise 8
Possible answers:

1 Secondary employment fell steadily between 1980 and 2010.
2 Primary employment fell sharply / noticeably between 1980 and 1985.
3 Tertiary employment grew marginally / somewhat between 1980 and 2000.
4 Primary employment fell steadily between 1985 and 2010.
5 Teriary employment grew sharply / noticeably between 2000 and 2010.

Exercise 9

Verb	Noun
modify	modification
decrease	decrease
increase	increase
distort	distortion
incorporate	incorporation
rise	rise
include	inclusion
decline	decline
grow	growth
improve	improvement
expand	expansion

Exercise 10
1 steady
2 diminished
3 expansion
4 marginal
5 inclusion
6 modification
7 sharp
8 dramatically

Exercise 11
1 c   2 a   3 b   4 e   5 d

Chapter 10

Exercise 1
1 Time series graph
2 Multiple bar chart
3 Multiple bar chart
4 Time series graph

Exercise 2

1 longer

2 better

3 happier

4 more motivated

5 more accomplished

6 higher

7 more technological

8 deeper

Exercise 3

2 … sleep longer than adults.

3 … travelled further than group A.

4 … lowered their cholesterol further than group B.

5 … scored lower in the test than in coursework.

6 … were more stressed than teachers.

Exercise 4

1 much more emotional

2 far more likely

3 slightly modified

4 considerably lower

5 significantly better

6 a little slower

Exercise 5

1 the happier

2 the more negative

3 the more carefully

4 the more difficult

5 the harder

6 the greater

Exercise 6

1 similarities between

2 A comparison of

3 similarities between / differences in

4 distinguish between

5 different from

Exercise 7

Similarities	Differences
both	however
in comparison to	instead
as well as	in contrast
also	while
compared with	rather than
likewise	

Exercise 8

2 Some people might feel that the obsession with attractiveness is a relatively new phenomenon. However, it is actually a biological factor determining survival and success.

3 The face conveys information about age, health and also fertility.

4 Good skin condition is a reliable indicator of a strong immune system. Likewise, a symmetrical face is perceived as a sign of good health.

5 People often think of certain physical features as key to attractiveness, whereas research now indicates that unique features might make people more attractive.

Exercise 9

1 b 2 c 3 a 4 c 5 b 6 a 7 b

Exercise 10

1 most expensive   3 easiest

2 most careful   4 most significant

Exercise 11

1 Arguably the most important

2 Potentially the most problematic

3 Perhaps the most interesting

4 possibly the most threatened

5 probably … most popular

Exercise 12

1 would

2 ought to

3 seemingly

4 roughly

5 broadly speaking

6 in a sense

7 in some respects

8 it is claimed

9 it is considered

10 it could be argued that

Chapter 11

Exercise 1

1 Negatively correlated

2 Positively correlated

3 Negatively correlated

4 Not correlated

5 Positively correlated

Exercise 2

1 positively

2 increases / rises

3 increases

4 negatively

5 decreases

6 increases

Exercise 3

1 b   2 c   3 f   4 a   5 d   6 e

Exercise 4

2 refer to

3 reveals links between

4 associate with

5 bring together

6 correlate ... with

Exercise 5

1 b   2 a   3 a   4 b   5 a   6 b

7 b   8 a

Exercise 6

Quality of the data	Gathering the data	Interpreting the data
comprehensive accurate empirical	organize analyse record	reflects demonstrates indicates interpret shows

Exercise 7

1 positive

2 positive

3 positive

4 negative

5 negative

6 positive

7 negative

Chapter 12

Exercise 1

There are no data values or percentages displayed on the pie chart on the left-hand side, making it difficult to interpret the information and draw accurate conclusions.

The tilted three-dimensional perspective distorts the way in which we compare the relative sizes of the sections in the chart; it looks as though approximately the same percentage of people cycle to work as those who take the train, but the pie chart on the right clearly shows that just over twice the number of people cycle compared to those who travel by train.

Exercise 2

Every diagram should include: informative labels on both axes or all sections of the diagram, all available data, a key to distinguish between categories or data sets, and a meaningful title.

Exercise 3

1 As a result of increased prices, people are continually making alternative purchases.

2 On account of bad weather, analysts claim up to $5 billion is lost annually.

3 Adverse economic conditions have affected a range of commodities. Hence, prices have rapidly increased.

4 In the previous decade there has been a significant increase in the numbers of graduates worldwide. In part this is due to the expansion of university education in developing economies.

5 Many medical advances are actually made by companies. Therefore, diseases and conditions that are likely to generate a profit are targeted.

6 Fifteen questionnaires were spoiled or incomplete and consequently discarded from the analysis.

Exercise 4

1 c   2 g   3 a   4 e   5 d   6 b   7 f

Exercise 5

1 factor

2 impact

3 blame

4 origin

5 relationship

6 attributed

7 contribute

Exercise 6

1 e   2 b   3 a   4 d   5 c

Exercise 7

1 b   2 b   3 a   4 a   5 b   6 a

Exercise 8

1 certainly

2 Typically / Generally / Largely

3 Typically / Generally / Largely

4 Apparently

5 probably

6 Largely / Typically / Generally

Exercise 9

1 negative

2 positive

3 positive

4 positive

5 negative

6 positive

7 negative

8 positive

Exercise 10

1 validity

2 solid

3 notable

4 underlined

5 limited

6 challenges

Exercise 11

1 attempted

2 In conclusion

3 balance

4 In brief

5 final